BASIC C#.NET

*Learn how to use Access and SQL
Server databases to create ASP,
ASPX, HTA, HTML Webpages*

Richard Edwards

INTRODUCTION

Some very exciting times!

I harbor the belief that all people who want to learn a computer language and do something with it that is both satisfying and lucrative at the same time, will find a way to make that happen.

But, yep, there's always a but somewhere along the line, the question is not whether you can do it or not but who is going to believe you when you say you can?

Well, I think we can all agree that degrees are fast become more a problem than a solution, right?

I mean after all, my daughter who has a degree in Computer Sciences is finding it hard to land a job. Not because she is a female or smart. But because she bought into the belief that getting a degree will gain her a front seat access pass to a job.

Truth is, it's a piece of paper that says you went to school and graduated. It doesn't come with a money back guarantee that you will ever land a job as a programmer.

Now, imagine, for a moment that you are a person looking for an **SDET.** Which means he or she is looking for a Software **Development** Engineer in Test. This type of job description can mean you are creating a program and testing it for functionality as you go, or you know how to code up a project and you know how to test it.

One leans heavy on the development process while the other has more emphasis on the testing. It is very rare that a developer is as enthusiastic about performing the destructive aspects of testing his or her creations. So, most of the time we weed out those jobs that place more time on testing than the need for someone to design the project and perform black box testing.

So, a job description looks promising.

Who do you think Microsoft is going to hire? The person with a Computer Science Degree or the person who knows how to code up a program that spits out html pages using C#.Net and connects to a SQL Server backend to grace the webpages with data?

While it might not be the highest paying job I would ever go for, I'm pretty sure I'm going to win the interview and land the job.

The big question, however, is just how much experience without a Computer Science degree is needed to earn the right to look for a job? I mean, after all, colleges do teach some C#.Net coding skills, don't they?

Truth is, a Computer Science degree is more than 75 credit hours – over 75% of the college credit hours dealing with English, Math, Humanities and so forth and so on. So, just how ready are people with Computer Science degrees ready to deal with real world programming issues?

They aren't. In fact, even if a school had 3 12-hour courses writing C#.Net code worth 3 credit hours each, the chances of them knowing enough about HTML and SQL Server and combining them so that they worked interactively – what the job description I created would require – it is doubtful that any of them could, in fact, go head to head with someone who knew HTML, could add CSS to them to make the pages look awesome and could write the C#.Net coder to make all of it work seamlessly with SQL Server as the back end database driving the HTML!

You, on the other hand have me to help you through the process of learning HTML, the necessary C#.Net code to make this interact with the HTML and SQL Server and, in the end, hopefully, feel confident enough to apply for such jobs.

Notice I didn't say I promise that you will land a job. As the old saying goes, "you can lead a horse to water, but you can't make it drink.", so it is with landing a job knowing what is being covered in this book. I can show you what you need to know, the rest of it is up to you to write the code, test it, and fix your bugs until the code works flawlessly and seamlessly.

HTML

Divide and conquer

HTML or Hyper Text Markup Language really hasn't changed much since the time it was created back in 1990. Currently, there are roughly 250 tags.

Even at that, a lot of tags aren't used by most HTML programmers. The most popular being tables, links, images, scripts and header information designed to get you visibility from the search engines.

My method of organizing HTML is to divide the tags into two categories: Page Layout and text decoration.

For example, text tags can include:

```
<abbr>
<address>
<b>
<bdi>
<bdo>
<blockquote>
<center>
<cite>
<code>
<del>
<emp>
<font>
<i>
<pre>
<u>
<small>
<strike>
```

Of course, there are more. But the most used for page layout are:

```
<!DOCTYPE html>
<html>
<head>
<title></title>
<meta>
<script>
</head>
<body>
<form>
<input>
<a>
<img>
<table>
<tr>
<thead>
<tbody>
<th>
<td>
</tr>
</table>
<ol><li></li></ol>
<ul><li></li></ul>
<p>
<br/>
<div>
</html>
```

As a matter of fact, the above tags are the tags that the webpages in the world use. It is the attributes – which we programmers like calling properties that combined with Cascading Stylesheets which make them work and look good on the internet.

Let's go with an example.

```
<table>
<tr>
    <th>First Name</th>
    <th>MI</th>
    <th>Last Name</th>
</tr>
```

```
<tr>
        <td>Richard</td>
        <td>T</td>
        <td>Edwards</td>
    </tr>
    </table>
```

If you are new to what these tags are and what they mean, the <table> tag tells the browser that a table of organized tags is coming its way. The <tr> tells the browser that a table row of either <th> table headers or <td> table data will follow.

Now there is a pair of tags used that assures that tables that are self-created via a database connection only repeats the data and not the table names or <th> tags. That would look like this:

```
<table>
<thead>
<tr>
    <th>First Name</th>
    <th>MI</th>
    <th>Last Name</th>
</tr>
</thead>
<tbody>
<tr>
        <td>Richard</td>
        <td>T</td>
        <td>Edwards</td>
</tr>
</tbody>
</table>
```

There is also a <tfoot> tag which is used for things like tallies, sums or totals based on the end user's need to know what all those rows that blurred past your boss's eyes add up to. (which is probably the only thing he or she really wanted to see in the first place, but you just had to show off your html skills, didn't you?)

IN DEPTH VIEW OF TABLE TAGS

Because table tags a so widely used and often their abilities least understood or even used, I felt it important to give these tags their a due and give them a couple of pages worth of visibility.

When you add a table tag or element as it is called in the HTML Document Object Model (DOM), you have tag specific attributes you can set. You also have built in event driven tags.

The property attribute tags are the following:

```
border
cellpadding
cellspacing
class
dir
frame
id
lang
rules
style
summary
title
visible
```

The event attribute tags are the following:

```
onclick
ondatabinding
ondblclick
ondisposed
oninit
onkeydown
onkeypress
onkeyup
onload
onmousedown
onmousemove
onmouseout
onmouseover
onmouseup
onprerender
onunload
```

Let's talk about some of the property attributes first.

border

This one gets used a lot because it renders the table two ways that most people accept as a report or table. Border=0 gives the table the feel of a report. Border = 1 or above gives the table the feel of a table.

cellpadding

Cellpadding adds additional space between the ending and the beginning of each </th><th> or </td><td> tags. This enhances user experience and makes it easier on the eyes to read.

cellspacing

Cellspacing adds spaces between the beginning and ending characters in between the TH or TD tags. An example of this would be like this:
    <th>First Name</th>
Specifying cellspacing as 2, the above would be the same thing as:
    <th> First Name </th>

class

The class attribute is CSS on steroids. If you type:
    <style type= "text/css ">
    table.main
    {
        border-color: navy;
        border-width: 2px;
        text-align: left
    }

```css
.solid
{
    border-style: solid;
}
.double
{
    border-style: double;
}
.ridge
{
    border-style: ridge;
}
.inset
{
    border-style: inset;
}
.groove
{
    border-style: groove;
}
.dashed
{
    border-style: dashed;
}
.dotted
{
    border-style: dotted;
}
.outset
{
    border-style: outset;
}
</style>
```

You now have a way to add the border style to all HTML tags or elements that support the class attribute. The code looks like this:

```
<!DOCTYPE html>
<html>
  <head>
    <title>First Page</title>
    <style type= "text/css" >
    table.main
    {
       color: navy;
       font-size:12px;
       font-family: Cambria, serif;
       border-color: navy;
       border-width: 2px;
       text-align: left
    }
    .solid
    {
       border-style: solid;
    }
    .double
    {
       border-style: double;
    }
    .ridge
    {
       border-style: ridge;
    }
    .inset
    {
       border-style: inset;
    }
```

```
    .groove
    {
        border-style: groove;
    }
    .dashed
    {
        border-style: dashed;
    }
    .dotted
    {
        border-style: dotted;
    }
    .outset
    {
        border-style: outset;
    }
    </style>
  </head>
  <body>
    <table    class    =    "table.main    double"    frame="both"    rules="all"
cellpadding="3px">
        <thead>
          <tr>
            <th>First Name</th>
            <th>MI</th>
            <th>Last Name</th>
          </tr>
        </thead>
        <tbody>
          <tr>
            <td>Richard</td>
                <td>T</td>
            <td>Edwards</td>
```

```
        </tr>
      </tbody>
    </table>
  </body>
</html>
```

And it produces this:

First Name	MI	Last Name
Richard	T	Edwards

When we add the following to the stylesheet:

```
th
{
    color: white;
    background-color: navy;
    font-size:12px;
    font-family:Calibri, Sans-Serif
}
td
{
    color: black;
    background-color: white;
    font-size:12px;
    font-family:Calibri, Sans-Serif
}
```

We get this:

First Name	MI	Last Name
Richard	T	Edwards

And when we modify the table attributes to this:

<table border=0 cellpadding="3px">

We get this:

So, as you can see, our existing CSS stylesheet provides us with a lot of visual power and effects. We're going to be doing a lot more but before we do, we want to first create a database and table, populate it with information and then present what we discovered using the code we have created here.

CREATING THE DATABASE

Let's keep it simple

What is the one resource on your machine that is free and can be used to create a database that we know will work and create something that your system administrator can appreciate – perhaps, even you can, too?

The answer is WMI. We can easily create an Access Database, populate a table with information about BIOS, Internet Connection Information, Processes and Services. And that isn't even scratching the surface.

So, we'll use it to gather some information about the local machine that you are on and then you can try some of the other classes. Once you're comfortable with the Access Database, we'll create the same thing in SQL Server.

With that said, let's create the code needed to gather information from Win32_Service:

```
using System;
using System.Collections.Generic;
using System.ComponentModel;
using System.Data;
using System.Drawing;
using System.Linq;
using System.Text;
using System.Windows.Forms;
using System.Management;
using System.Security;

namespace WindowsFormsApplication1
```

```csharp
{
    public partial class Form1 : Form
    {
        public Form1()
        {
            InitializeComponent();
        }

        private void Form1_Load(object sender, EventArgs e)
        {
            //first let's create a Connection Options
            ConnectionOptions cops = new ConnectionOptions();
            cops.Authentication =
AuthenticationLevel.PacketPrivacy;
            cops.Impersonation = ImpersonationLevel.Impersonate;
            cops.Locale = "MS0409";

            ////the only time you will need to add credentials is
when you connect to a remote machine
            //cops.Username = "";

            //SecureString ss = new SecureString();
            ////example here is Snoopy
            //String pwd = "Snoopy";

            //for(int x=0; x < pwd.Length-1;x++)
            //{
            //    ss.AppendChar(pwd[x]);
            //}
            //cops.SecurePassword = ss;



            //Now, let's create a Path
            ManagementPath path = new ManagementPath();
            path.ClassName = "Win32_Service";
            path.NamespacePath = "root\\cimv2";
            path.Server= "LocalHost";

            //now, let's create a scope
            ManagementScope scope = new ManagementScope(path,
cops);
            scope.Connect();

            //Now, let's create a ManagementObjectSearcher
```

```csharp
            ManagementObjectSearcher mos = new
ManagementObjectSearcher();
            mos.Scope.Path = scope.Path;
            mos.Query.QueryString = "Select * From
Win32_Service";
            ManagementObjectCollection moc = mos.Get();
            ManagementObjectCollection.ManagementObjectEnumerator
mocEnum = moc.GetEnumerator();
            while (mocEnum.MoveNext())
            {
                ManagementBaseObject mo = mocEnum.Current;
                PropertyDataCollection props = mo.Properties;
                PropertyDataCollection.PropertyDataEnumerator
propEnum = props.GetEnumerator();
                while (propEnum.MoveNext())
                {
                    PropertyData prop = propEnum.Current;
                    Console.Out.WriteLine(prop.Name + " = " +
GetValue(prop.Name, mo));
                }
            }
        }

        private System.String GetValue(System.String Name,
ManagementBaseObject mo)
        {
            int pos = 0;
            System.String tName = Name + " = ";
            System.String tempstr = mo.GetText(TextFormat.Mof);
            pos = tempstr.IndexOf(tName);
            if (pos > -1)
            {
                pos = pos + tName.Length;
                tempstr = tempstr.Substring(pos, tempstr.Length -
pos);

                pos = tempstr.IndexOf(";");
                tempstr = tempstr.Substring(0, pos);
                tempstr = tempstr.Replace("\"", "");
                tempstr = tempstr.Replace("{", "");
                tempstr = tempstr.Replace("}", "");
                if (mo.Properties[Name].Type == CimType.DateTime
&& tempstr.Length > 14)
                {
                    return tempstr.Substring(5, 2) + "/" +
tempstr.Substring(7, 2) + "/" + tempstr.Substring(0, 4) + " " +
```

```
tempstr.Substring(9, 2) + ":" + tempstr.Substring(11, 2) + ":" +
tempstr.Substring(13, 2);
                }
                else
                {
                    return tempstr;
                }
            }
            else
            {
                return "";
            }
        }

    }
}
```

What all of this does is assure that we are getting the property information and property values as expected. The code below completes the creation of the database, table and fields and then populates the fields with the values.

```
using System;
using System.Collections.Generic;
using System.ComponentModel;
using System.Data;
using System.Drawing;
using System.Linq;
using System.Text;
using System.Windows.Forms;
using System.Management;
using System.Security;
using ADOX;
using ADODB;


namespace WindowsFormsApplication1
{
    public partial class Form1 : Form
    {
        public Form1()
        {
            InitializeComponent();
```

```csharp
        }

        private void Form1_Load(object sender, EventArgs e)
        {
            //first let's create a Connection Options
            ConnectionOptions cops = new ConnectionOptions();
            cops.Authentication =
AuthenticationLevel.PacketPrivacy;
            cops.Impersonation = ImpersonationLevel.Impersonate;
            cops.Locale = "MS0409";

            ////the only time you will need to add credentials is
when you connect to a remote machine
            //cops.Username = "";

            //SecureString ss = new SecureString();
            ////example here is Snoopy
            //String pwd = "Snoopy";

            //for(int x=0; x < pwd.Length-1;x++)
            //{
            //    ss.AppendChar(pwd[x]);
            //}
            //cops.SecurePassword = ss;


            //Now, let's create a Path
            ManagementPath path = new ManagementPath();
            path.ClassName = "Win32_Service";
            path.NamespacePath = "root\\cimv2";
            path.Server= "LocalHost";

            //now, let's create a scope
            ManagementScope scope = new ManagementScope(path,
cops);
            scope.Connect();

            //Now, let's create a ManagementObjectSearcher
            ManagementObjectSearcher mos = new
ManagementObjectSearcher();
            mos.Scope.Path = scope.Path;
            mos.Query.QueryString = "Select * From
Win32_Service";
            ManagementObjectCollection moc = mos.Get();
```

```csharp
            ManagementObjectCollection.ManagementObjectEnumerator
mocEnum = moc.GetEnumerator();
            while (mocEnum.MoveNext())
            {
                ManagementBaseObject mo = mocEnum.Current;
                PropertyDataCollection props = mo.Properties;
                Create_The_Database_And_Table("Service",
"Properties", props);
                break;
            }
            mocEnum.Reset();

            Populate_The_Table("Service", "Properties", mocEnum);

        }
        private void Create_The_Database_And_Table(string
databasename, string tablename, PropertyDataCollection props)
        {
            Catalog ocat = new Catalog();
            ocat.Create("Provider=Microsoft.Jet.Oledb.4.0;Data
Source=" + System.Environment.CurrentDirectory + "\\" +
databasename + ".mdb");
            Table otable = new Table();
            otable.Name = tablename;
            foreach(PropertyData prop in props)
            {
                ADOX.Column oColumn = new ADOX.Column();
                oColumn.Name = prop.Name;
                oColumn.Type = ADOX.DataTypeEnum.adLongVarWChar;
                oColumn.Attributes =
ColumnAttributesEnum.adColNullable;
                otable.Columns.Append(oColumn);
            }
            ocat.Tables.Append(otable);
        }
        private void Populate_The_Table(string databasename,
string tablename,
ManagementObjectCollection.ManagementObjectEnumerator mocEnum)
        {

            ADODB.Recordset rs = new ADODB.Recordset();

rs.let_ActiveConnection("Provider=Microsoft.Jet.Oledb.4.0;Data
Source=" + System.Environment.CurrentDirectory + "\\" +
databasename + ".mdb");
```

```csharp
            rs.LockType = LockTypeEnum.adLockPessimistic;
            rs.CursorLocation = CursorLocationEnum.adUseClient;
            rs.Let_Source("Select * From " + tablename);
            rs.Open();

            int x = 0;

            while (mocEnum.MoveNext())
            {
                rs.AddNew();
                ManagementBaseObject mo = mocEnum.Current;
                PropertyDataCollection props = mo.Properties;
                PropertyDataCollection.PropertyDataEnumerator
propEnum = props.GetEnumerator();
                while (propEnum.MoveNext())
                {
                    PropertyData prop = propEnum.Current;
                    try
                    {
                        rs.Fields[x].Value = GetValue(prop.Name,
mo);

                        x = x + 1;
                    }
                    catch(Exception ex)
                    {

                    }

                }
                x = 0;
                rs.Update();
            }

        }
        private System.String GetValue(System.String Name,
ManagementBaseObject mo)
        {
            int pos = 0;
            System.String tName = Name + " = ";
            System.String tempstr = mo.GetText(TextFormat.Mof);
            pos = tempstr.IndexOf(tName);
            if (pos > -1)
            {
                pos = pos + tName.Length;
```

```
                    tempstr = tempstr.Substring(pos, tempstr.Length -
pos);
                    pos = tempstr.IndexOf(";");
                    tempstr = tempstr.Substring(0, pos);
                    tempstr = tempstr.Replace("\"", "");
                    tempstr = tempstr.Replace("{", "");
                    tempstr = tempstr.Replace("}", "");
                    if (mo.Properties[Name].Type == CimType.DateTime
&& tempstr.Length > 14)
                    {
                        return tempstr.Substring(5, 2) + "/" +
tempstr.Substring(7, 2) + "/" + tempstr.Substring(0, 4) + " " +
tempstr.Substring(9, 2) + ":" + tempstr.Substring(11, 2) + ":" +
tempstr.Substring(13, 2);
                    }
                    else
                    {
                        return tempstr;
                    }
                }
                else
                {
                    return "";
                }
            }

        }
}
```

I also added a couple of things to this code I generally don't have to do. The first one setting the oColumn.Attributes = ColumnAttributesEnum.adColNullable. The second one was adding the try, catch block of code to the addnew/update routine.

I did this because someone at Microsoft decided that their additional field names and values didn't have to conform to the expected WMI standards, and those two additional fields causes the routine to fail. It also causes the values on that row to not line up properly to their correct fields either.

Despite all of this, after creating the database and opening it up in Access, this is what I saw:

AcceptPause	AcceptStop	Caption	CheckPoint	CreationClas	DelayedAuto	Description	Desktopinte	DisplayName
FALSE	TRUE	System Event N	0	Win32_Service	FALSE	Monitors system events and notifies subscribers to COM+ Event Sys	FALSE	System Event N
FALSE	FALSE	Sensor Data Se	0	Win32_Service	FALSE	Delivers data from a variety of sensors	FALSE	Sensor Data Se
FALSE	FALSE	Sensor Service	0	Win32_Service	FALSE	A service for sensors that manages different sensors' functionality.	FALSE	Sensor Service
FALSE	FALSE	Sensor Monitor	0	Win32_Service	FALSE	Monitors various sensors in order to expose data and adapt to syste	FALSE	Sensor Monitor
FALSE	FALSE	Remote Deskto	0	Win32_Service	FALSE	Remote Desktop Configuration service (RDCS) is responsible for all R	FALSE	Remote Deskto
FALSE	FALSE	Internet Conne	0	Win32_Service	FALSE	Provides network address translation, addressing, name resolution :	FALSE	Internet Conne
FALSE	TRUE	Shell Hardware	0	Win32_Service	FALSE	Provides notifications for AutoPlay hardware events.	FALSE	Shell Hardware
FALSE	FALSE	Microsoft Store	0	Win32_Service	FALSE	Host service for the Microsoft Storage Spaces management provider	FALSE	Microsoft Store
FALSE	FALSE	SNMP Trap	0	Win32_Service	FALSE	Receives trap messages generated by local or remote Simple Networ	FALSE	SNMP Trap
FALSE	TRUE	Print Spooler	0	Win32_Service	FALSE	This service spools print jobs and handles interaction with the printe	TRUE	Print Spooler
FALSE	FALSE	Software Prote	0	Win32_Service	TRUE	Enables the download, installation and enforcement of digital license	FALSE	Software Prote
FALSE	FALSE	SQL Server Age	0	Win32_Service	FALSE	Executes jobs, monitors SQL Server, fires alerts, and allows automati	FALSE	SQL Server Age
FALSE	FALSE	SQL Server Bro	0	Win32_Service	FALSE	Provides SQL Server connection information to client computers.	FALSE	SQL Server Bro
FALSE	TRUE	SQL Server VSS	0	Win32_Service	FALSE	Provides the interface to backup/restore Microsoft SQL server throu	FALSE	SQL Server VSS
FALSE	TRUE	SSDP Discovery	0	Win32_Service	FALSE	Discovers networked devices and services that use the SSDP discove	FALSE	SSDP Discovery
FALSE	FALSE	Secure Socket T	0	Win32_Service	FALSE	Provides support for the Secure Socket Tunneling Protocol (SSTP) to	FALSE	Secure Socket T
FALSE	TRUE	State Repositor	0	Win32_Service	FALSE	Provides required infrastructure support for the application model.	FALSE	State Repositor
TRUE	TRUE	Windows Imag	0	Win32_Service	FALSE	Provides Image acquisition services for scanners and cameras	FALSE	Windows Imag
FALSE	FALSE	Storage Service	0	Win32_Service	FALSE	Provides enabling services for storage settings and external storage :	FALSE	Storage Service
FALSE	FALSE	Spot Verifier	0	Win32_Service	FALSE	Verifies potential file system corruptions.	FALSE	Spot Verifier
FALSE	TRUE	Microsoft Soft	0	Win32_Service	FALSE	Manages software-based volume shadow copies taken by the Volur	FALSE	Microsoft Soft
FALSE	FALSE	Superfetch	0	Win32_Service	FALSE	Maintains and improves system performance over time.	FALSE	Superfetch
FALSE	TRUE	System Events	0	Win32_Service	FALSE	Coordinates execution of background work for WinRT application. If	FALSE	System Events

Record: 14 ◄ 1 of 217 ► ►I ►* 🔍 No Filter Search ◄

There are 217 rows with 27 fields, and it took about a second to create the database, table and fields and then populate the table. That's pretty darn fast in my books.

Just remember a couple of things when using the code. It assumes you have no database, no table and no fields. There's also a hard-wired database name and tablename. If you use a different class, drop the win32_ on the class and use the rest of the name as your databasename.

CREATING THE HTML

The easy way

The easiest and simplest of ways to approach this segment of the webpage development process is to eliminate everything but the table code.

Unless we are changing the HTML before and after the table, the only part of the HTML webpage that will change dynamically will be the table view. So, how do we do this?

Well, the easiest way is to use Visual Studio 2010 and comment out all the html up to the table. This is what I did:

Added a class and then added the code below:

```
using System;
using System.Collections.Generic;
using System.Linq;
using System.Text;
using Scripting;
using System.Data;
using System.Data.OleDb;
namespace WindowsFormsApplication1
{
    class Class1
    {
        TextStream txtstream;
        public void Start_The_Show(string fName)
        {
            FileSystemObject fso = new FileSystemObject();
            txtstream = fso.OpenTextFile(fName,
IOMode.ForWriting, true, Tristate.TristateUseDefault);
            txtstream.WriteLine("<!DOCTYPE html>");
            txtstream.WriteLine("<html>");
```

```
            txtstream.WriteLine("        <head>");
            txtstream.WriteLine("        <title>First Page</title>");
            txtstream.WriteLine("        <style type=\"text/css\">");
            txtstream.WriteLine("        th");
            txtstream.WriteLine("        {");
            txtstream.WriteLine("            color: white;");
            txtstream.WriteLine("            background-color: navy;");
            txtstream.WriteLine("            font-size:12px;");
            txtstream.WriteLine("            font-family:Calibri, Sans-Serif;");
            txtstream.WriteLine("            white-space: nowrap;");
            txtstream.WriteLine("        }");
            txtstream.WriteLine("        td");
            txtstream.WriteLine("        {");
            txtstream.WriteLine("            color: black;");
            txtstream.WriteLine("            background-color: white;");
            txtstream.WriteLine("            font-size:12px;");
            txtstream.WriteLine("            font-family:Calibri, Sans-Serif;");
            txtstream.WriteLine("            white-space: nowrap;");
            txtstream.WriteLine("        }");
            txtstream.WriteLine("        table.main");
            txtstream.WriteLine("        {");
            txtstream.WriteLine("            border-color: navy;");
            txtstream.WriteLine("            border-width: 2px;");
            txtstream.WriteLine("            text-align: left");
            txtstream.WriteLine("        }");
            txtstream.WriteLine("        .solid");
            txtstream.WriteLine("        {");
            txtstream.WriteLine("            border-style: solid;");
            txtstream.WriteLine("        }");
            txtstream.WriteLine("        .double");
            txtstream.WriteLine("        {");
            txtstream.WriteLine("            border-style: double;");
            txtstream.WriteLine("        }");
```

```csharp
            txtstream.WriteLine("          .ridge");
            txtstream.WriteLine("          {");
            txtstream.WriteLine("               border-style:
ridge;");
            txtstream.WriteLine("          }");
            txtstream.WriteLine("          .inset");
            txtstream.WriteLine("          {");
            txtstream.WriteLine("               border-style:
inset;");
            txtstream.WriteLine("          }");
            txtstream.WriteLine("          .groove");
            txtstream.WriteLine("          {");
            txtstream.WriteLine("               border-style:
groove;");
            txtstream.WriteLine("          }");
            txtstream.WriteLine("          .dashed");
            txtstream.WriteLine("          {");
            txtstream.WriteLine("               border-style:
dashed;");
            txtstream.WriteLine("          }");
            txtstream.WriteLine("          .dotted");
            txtstream.WriteLine("          {");
            txtstream.WriteLine("               border-style:
dotted;");
            txtstream.WriteLine("          }");
            txtstream.WriteLine("          .outset");
            txtstream.WriteLine("          {");
            txtstream.WriteLine("               border-style:
outset;");
            txtstream.WriteLine("          }");
            txtstream.WriteLine("          </style>");
            txtstream.WriteLine("     </head>");
            txtstream.WriteLine("     <body>");
        }
        public void Write_The_Table_To_HTML(string cnstr, string
tablename)
        {

            OleDbDataAdapter da = new OleDbDataAdapter("Select *
From " + tablename, cnstr);
            System.Data.DataTable dt = new
System.Data.DataTable();
            da.Fill(dt);
```

```csharp
            txtstream.WriteLine("          <table border=0
cellpadding=\"3px\">");
            txtstream.WriteLine("                <thead>");
            txtstream.WriteLine("                  <tr>");
            foreach(System.Data.DataColumn dc in dt.Columns)
            {
                txtstream.WriteLine("                      <th>" +
dc.Caption + "</th>");
            }
            txtstream.WriteLine("                  </tr>");
            txtstream.WriteLine("                </thead>");
            txtstream.WriteLine("          <tbody>");
            foreach(System.Data.DataRow dr in dt.Rows)
            {
                txtstream.WriteLine("                    <tr>");
                foreach(System.Data.DataColumn dc in dt.Columns)
                {
                    try
                    {
                        txtstream.WriteLine("
<td>" + dr[dc.Caption].ToString() + "</td>");
                    }
                    catch (Exception ex)
                    {
                        txtstream.WriteLine("
<td></td>");
                    }

                }
                txtstream.WriteLine("                        </tr>");
            }
            txtstream.WriteLine("            </tbody>");
            txtstream.WriteLine("        </table>");
        }
        public void End_The_Show()
        {
            txtstream.WriteLine("      </body>");
            txtstream.WriteLine("</html>");
            txtstream.Close();
        }
    }
}
```

And the results:

AcceptPause	AcceptStop	Caption	CheckPoint	CreationClassName	DelayedAutoStart
FALSE	TRUE	System Event Notification Service	0	Win32_Service	FALSE
FALSE	FALSE	Sensor Data Service	0	Win32_Service	FALSE
FALSE	FALSE	Sensor Service	0	Win32_Service	FALSE
FALSE	FALSE	Sensor Monitoring Service	0	Win32_Service	FALSE
FALSE	FALSE	Remote Desktop Configuration	0	Win32_Service	FALSE
FALSE	FALSE	Internet Connection Sharing (ICS)	0	Win32_Service	FALSE
FALSE	TRUE	Shell Hardware Detection	0	Win32_Service	FALSE
FALSE	FALSE	Microsoft Storage Spaces SMP	0	Win32_Service	FALSE
FALSE	FALSE	SNMP Trap	0	Win32_Service	FALSE
FALSE	TRUE	Print Spooler	0	Win32_Service	FALSE
FALSE	FALSE	Software Protection	0	Win32_Service	TRUE
FALSE	FALSE	SQL Server Agent (SQLEXPRESS)	0	Win32_Service	FALSE

This is what the report would look like. Let's look at what the table would look like:

AcceptPause	AcceptStop	Caption	CheckPoint	CreationClassName	DelayedAutoStart
FALSE	TRUE	System Event Notification Service	0	Win32_Service	FALSE
FALSE	FALSE	Sensor Data Service	0	Win32_Service	FALSE
FALSE	FALSE	Sensor Service	0	Win32_Service	FALSE
FALSE	FALSE	Sensor Monitoring Service	0	Win32_Service	FALSE
FALSE	FALSE	Remote Desktop Configuration	0	Win32_Service	FALSE
FALSE	FALSE	Internet Connection Sharing (ICS)	0	Win32_Service	FALSE
FALSE	TRUE	Shell Hardware Detection	0	Win32_Service	FALSE
FALSE	FALSE	Microsoft Storage Spaces SMP	0	Win32_Service	FALSE
FALSE	FALSE	SNMP Trap	0	Win32_Service	FALSE
FALSE	TRUE	Print Spooler	0	Win32_Service	FALSE
FALSE	FALSE	Software Protection	0	Win32_Service	TRUE
FALSE	FALSE	SQL Server Agent (SQLEXPRESS)	0	Win32_Service	FALSE
FALSE	FALSE	SQL Server Browser	0	Win32_Service	FALSE
FALSE	TRUE	SQL Server VSS Writer	0	Win32_Service	FALSE
FALSE	TRUE	SSDP Discovery	0	Win32_Service	FALSE
FALSE	FALSE	Secure Socket Tunneling Protocol Service	0	Win32_Service	FALSE
FALSE	TRUE	State Repository Service	0	Win32_Service	FALSE
TRUE	TRUE	Windows Image Acquisition (WIA)	0	Win32_Service	FALSE
FALSE	FALSE	Storage Service	0	Win32_Service	FALSE

All well and good. What if we wanted to add HTML controls to the mix?

Fact is, I generally have around 10 I use but to be honest, a few of them aren't controls at all. They are tags: <div><span>. HTML5 has added a few new ones but they aren't things like textbox, textarea, listbox or combobox.

The problem is, the input type=textbox has been modified in such a way that trying to make it work like a textarea no longer works. In the case of using the

Win32_Service class, it especially doesn't work due to the max length the total amount of characters and numbers a row can visually handle.

AcceptPause	AcceptStop	Caption	CheckPoint	CreationClassName
FALSE	TRUE	System Event Notification Service	0	Win32_Service
FALSE	FALSE	Sensor Data Service	0	Win32_Service
FALSE	FALSE	Sensor Service	0	Win32_Service
FALSE	FALSE	Sensor Monitoring Service	0	Win32_Service
FALSE	FALSE	Remote Desktop Configuration	0	Win32_Service
FALSE	FALSE	Internet Connection Sharing (ICS)	0	Win32_Service
FALSE	TRUE	Shell Hardware Detection	0	Win32_Service
FALSE	FALSE	Microsoft Storage Spaces SMP	0	Win32_Service
FALSE	FALSE	SNMP Trap	0	Win32_Service
FALSE	TRUE	Print Spooler	0	Win32_Service
FALSE	FALSE	Software Protection	0	Win32_Service
FALSE	FALSE	SQL Server Agent (SQLEXPRESS)	0	Win32_Service
FALSE	FALSE	SQL Server Browser	0	Win32_Service
FALSE	TRUE	SQL Server VSS Writer	0	Win32_Service
FALSE	TRUE	SSDP Discovery	0	Win32_Service
FALSE	FALSE	Secure Socket Tunneling Protocol Ser	0	Win32_Service
FALSE	TRUE	State Repository Service	0	Win32_Service

So, if we used a textarea, would this help?

AcceptPause	AcceptStop	Caption	CheckPoint	CreationClassName
FALSE	TRUE	System Event Notification Service	0	Win32_Service
FALSE	FALSE	Sensor Data Service	0	Win32_Service
FALSE	FALSE	Sensor Service	0	Win32_Service
FALSE	FALSE	Sensor Monitoring Service	0	Win32_Service
FALSE	FALSE	Remote Desktop Configuration	0	Win32_Service
FALSE	FALSE	Internet Connection Sharing (ICS)	0	Win32_Service
FALSE	TRUE	Shell Hardware Detection	0	Win32_Service
FALSE	FALSE	Microsoft Storage Spaces SMP	0	Win32_Service
FALSE	FALSE	SNMP Trap	0	Win32_Service
FALSE	TRUE	Print Spooler	0	Win32_Service

Apparently, not.

Perhaps the Select tag will have a better tine at giving us what we want.

AcceptPause	AcceptStop	Caption	CheckPoint	CreationClassName	DelayedAutoStart
FALSE	TRUE	System Event Notification Service	0	Win32_Service	FALSE
FALSE	FALSE	Sensor Data Service	0	Win32_Service	FALSE
FALSE	FALSE	Sensor Service	0	Win32_Service	FALSE
FALSE	FALSE	Sensor Monitoring Service	0	Win32_Service	FALSE
FALSE	FALSE	Remote Desktop Configuration	0	Win32_Service	FALSE
FALSE	FALSE	Internet Connection Sharing (ICS)	0	Win32_Service	FALSE
FALSE	TRUE	Shell Hardware Detection	0	Win32_Service	FALSE
FALSE	FALSE	Microsoft Storage Spaces SMP	0	Win32_Service	FALSE
FALSE	FALSE	SNMP Trap	0	Win32_Service	FALSE
FALSE	TRUE	Print Spooler	0	Win32_Service	FALSE
FALSE	FALSE	Software Protection	0	Win32_Service	TRUE
FALSE	FALSE	SQL Server Agent (SQLEXPRESS)	0	Win32_Service	FALSE

This is what the report would look like. Let's look at what the table would look like:

AcceptPause	AcceptStop	Caption	CheckPoint	CreationClassName	DelayedAutoStart
FALSE	TRUE	System Event Notification Service	0	Win32_Service	FALSE
FALSE	FALSE	Sensor Data Service	0	Win32_Service	FALSE
FALSE	FALSE	Sensor Service	0	Win32_Service	FALSE
FALSE	FALSE	Sensor Monitoring Service	0	Win32_Service	FALSE
FALSE	FALSE	Remote Desktop Configuration	0	Win32_Service	FALSE
FALSE	FALSE	Internet Connection Sharing (ICS)	0	Win32_Service	FALSE
FALSE	TRUE	Shell Hardware Detection	0	Win32_Service	FALSE
FALSE	FALSE	Microsoft Storage Spaces SMP	0	Win32_Service	FALSE
FALSE	FALSE	SNMP Trap	0	Win32_Service	FALSE
FALSE	TRUE	Print Spooler	0	Win32_Service	FALSE
FALSE	FALSE	Software Protection	0	Win32_Service	TRUE
FALSE	FALSE	SQL Server Agent (SQLEXPRESS)	0	Win32_Service	FALSE
FALSE	FALSE	SQL Server Browser	0	Win32_Service	FALSE
FALSE	TRUE	SQL Server VSS Writer	0	Win32_Service	FALSE
FALSE	TRUE	SSDP Discovery	0	Win32_Service	FALSE
FALSE	FALSE	Secure Socket Tunneling Protocol Service	0	Win32_Service	FALSE
FALSE	TRUE	State Repository Service	0	Win32_Service	FALSE
TRUE	TRUE	Windows Image Acquisition (WIA)	0	Win32_Service	FALSE
FALSE	FALSE	Storage Service	0	Win32_Service	FALSE

All well and good. What if we wanted to add HTML controls to the mix?

Fact is, I generally have around 10 I use but to be honest, a few of them aren't controls at all. They are tags: <div><span>. HTML5 has added a few new ones but they aren't things like textbox, textarea, listbox or combobox.

The problem is, the input type=textbox has been modified in such a way that trying to make it work like a textarea no longer works. In the case of using the

Win32_Service class, it especially doesn't work due to the max length the total amount of characters and numbers a row can visually handle.

AcceptPause	AcceptStop	Caption	CheckPoint	CreationClassName
FALSE	TRUE	System Event Notification Service	0	Win32_Service
FALSE	FALSE	Sensor Data Service	0	Win32_Service
FALSE	FALSE	Sensor Service	0	Win32_Service
FALSE	FALSE	Sensor Monitoring Service	0	Win32_Service
FALSE	FALSE	Remote Desktop Configuration	0	Win32_Service
FALSE	FALSE	Internet Connection Sharing (ICS)	0	Win32_Service
FALSE	TRUE	Shell Hardware Detection	0	Win32_Service
FALSE	FALSE	Microsoft Storage Spaces SMP	0	Win32_Service
FALSE	FALSE	SNMP Trap	0	Win32_Service
FALSE	TRUE	Print Spooler	0	Win32_Service
FALSE	FALSE	Software Protection	0	Win32_Service
FALSE	FALSE	SQL Server Agent (SQLEXPRESS)	0	Win32_Service
FALSE	FALSE	SQL Server Browser	0	Win32_Service
FALSE	TRUE	SQL Server VSS Writer	0	Win32_Service
FALSE	TRUE	SSDP Discovery	0	Win32_Service
FALSE	FALSE	Secure Socket Tunneling Protocol Ser	0	Win32_Service
FALSE	TRUE	State Repository Service	0	Win32_Service

So, if we used a textarea, would this help?

AcceptPause	AcceptStop	Caption	CheckPoint	CreationClassName
FALSE	TRUE	System Event Notification Service	0	Win32_Service
FALSE	FALSE	Sensor Data Service	0	Win32_Service
FALSE	FALSE	Sensor Service	0	Win32_Service
FALSE	FALSE	Sensor Monitoring Service	0	Win32_Service
FALSE	FALSE	Remote Desktop Configuration	0	Win32_Service
FALSE	FALSE	Internet Connection Sharing (ICS)	0	Win32_Service
FALSE	TRUE	Shell Hardware Detection	0	Win32_Service
FALSE	FALSE	Microsoft Storage Spaces SMP	0	Win32_Service
FALSE	FALSE	SNMP Trap	0	Win32_Service
FALSE	TRUE	Print Spooler	0	Win32_Service

Apparently, not.

Perhaps the Select tag will have a better tine at giving us what we want.

AcceptPause	AcceptStop	Caption	CheckPoint	CreationClassName	DelayedAutoStart	Description	DesktopInteract
FALSE	TRUE	Sys	0	Win32_Service	FALSE	Monitor:	FALSE
FALSE	FALSE	Sen	0	Win32_Service	FALSE	Delivers	FALSE
FALSE	FALSE	Sen	0	Win32_Service	FALSE	A service	FALSE
FALSE	FALSE	Sen	0	Win32_Service	FALSE	Monitor:	FALSE
FALSE	FALSE	Ren	0	Win32_Service	FALSE	Remote I	FALSE
FALSE	FALSE	Inte	0	Win32_Service	FALSE	Provides	FALSE
FALSE	TRUE	She	0	Win32_Service	FALSE	Provides	FALSE
FALSE	FALSE	Mic	0	Win32_Service	FALSE	Host ser	FALSE
FALSE	FALSE	SNM	0	Win32_Service	FALSE	Receives	FALSE
FALSE	TRUE	Prir	0	Win32_Service	FALSE	This ser	TRUE
FALSE	FALSE	Soft	0	Win32_Service	TRUE	Enables	FALSE
FALSE	FALSE	SQL	0	Win32_Service	FALSE	Executes	FALSE
FALSE	FALSE	SQL	0	Win32_Service	FALSE	Provides	FALSE
FALSE	TRUE	SQL	0	Win32_Service	FALSE	Provides	FALSE

Nope, that didn't work either.

The real problem here is, indeed, the amount of information restricting the growth of the fields to their potential length using these controls based on the font size. Take a look at what happens when you do reduce the magnification of the browser's viewing area.

It might be hard to read at this point, but that very long line is the description doing exactly what it should be doing if the font could be reduced to that size.

The code is working, the css is doing its job. Is it the browser causing the issue? Want to see it work correctly?

Glad you do! Because, so did I. Hundreds of webpages later, none of the suggestions seemed to work. And then it dawned on me. If I write the code in ASP.Net, intel sense might just be able to help me find where everything went wrong and nudge me for the solution.

The fact is, all the css attributes that should have worked stopped working. In fact, it is almost as though Microsoft's newer browsers refuse to conform to anyone's standards. Why shouldn't nowrap work as it always did? Or the new CSS – new when it came out – version of nowrap work?

Luckily for me, I'm used to running size adjustments as a work around for years. Here's the code – a bit roughed in – that will resize any control to a specific size based on the field name length and the field value lengths.

```csharp
using System;
using System.Collections.Generic;
using System.Linq;
using System.Text;
using Scripting;
using System.Data;
using System.Data.OleDb;
namespace WindowsFormsApplication1
{
    class Class1
    {
        TextStream txtstream;
        public void Start_The_Show(string fName, string tablename)
        {
            FileSystemObject fso = new FileSystemObject();
            txtstream = fso.OpenTextFile(fName,
IOMode.ForWriting, true, Tristate.TristateUseDefault);
            //txtstream.WriteLine("<!DOCTYPE html>");
            txtstream.WriteLine("<html>");
            txtstream.WriteLine("    <head>");
            txtstream.WriteLine("<HTA:APPLICATION ");
            txtstream.WriteLine("NAVIGABLE = 'no' ");
            txtstream.WriteLine("ID = '" + tablename + "' ");
            txtstream.WriteLine("APPLICATIONNAME = '" + tablename
+ "' ");
            txtstream.WriteLine("SCROLL = 'no' ");
            txtstream.WriteLine("BorderStyle = 'normal' ");
            txtstream.WriteLine("SINGLEINSTANCE = 'yes' ");
            txtstream.WriteLine("WINDOWSTATE = 'maximize' ");
            txtstream.WriteLine("BORDER = 'thin' ");
            txtstream.WriteLine("CAPTION = 'yes' ");
            txtstream.WriteLine("MAXIMIZEBUTTON = 'no' ");
            txtstream.WriteLine("MINIMIZEBUTTON = 'no' ");
            txtstream.WriteLine("SHOWINTASKBAR = 'no'");
            txtstream.WriteLine("SYSMENU = 'yes'");
            txtstream.WriteLine(">");
            txtstream.WriteLine("        <title>First
Page</title>");
```

```
txtstream.WriteLine("                <style>");
txtstream.WriteLine("                th");
txtstream.WriteLine("                {");
txtstream.WriteLine("                  COLOR: white;");
txtstream.WriteLine("                  BACKGROUND-COLOR:
navy;");
txtstream.WriteLine("                  Font-family: Cambria,
serif;");
txtstream.WriteLine("                  FONT-SIZE: 12px;");
txtstream.WriteLine("                  text-align: left;");
txtstream.WriteLine("                  display:table-
cell;");
txtstream.WriteLine("                  white-Space:
nowrap;");
txtstream.WriteLine("                }");
txtstream.WriteLine("                td");
txtstream.WriteLine("                {");
txtstream.WriteLine("                  color: black;");
txtstream.WriteLine("                  background-color:
white;");
txtstream.WriteLine("                  font-size:10px;");
txtstream.WriteLine("                  font-family:Calibri,
Sans-Serif;");
txtstream.WriteLine("                  display:table-
cell;");
txtstream.WriteLine("                  text-align: left");
txtstream.WriteLine("                  white-space:
nowrap;");
txtstream.WriteLine("                }");
txtstream.WriteLine("                table.main");
txtstream.WriteLine("                {");
txtstream.WriteLine("                  border-color:
navy;");
txtstream.WriteLine("                  border-width: 2px;");
txtstream.WriteLine("                  text-align: left");
txtstream.WriteLine("                }");
txtstream.WriteLine("                input");
txtstream.WriteLine("                {");
txtstream.WriteLine("                  COLOR: black;");
txtstream.WriteLine("                  BACKGROUND-COLOR:
white;");
txtstream.WriteLine("                  Font-family: Cambria,
serif;");
txtstream.WriteLine("                  FONT-SIZE: 10px;");
txtstream.WriteLine("                  text-align: left");
```

```
        txtstream.WriteLine("          white-Space: nowrap;");
        txtstream.WriteLine("          width:100%;");
        txtstream.WriteLine("     }");
        txtstream.WriteLine("     .solid");
        txtstream.WriteLine("     {");
        txtstream.WriteLine("          width: 100%;");
        txtstream.WriteLine("          display: inline-block;");
        txtstream.WriteLine("     }");
        txtstream.WriteLine("     .double");
        txtstream.WriteLine("     {");
        txtstream.WriteLine("          border-style: double;");
        txtstream.WriteLine("     }");
        txtstream.WriteLine("     .ridge");
        txtstream.WriteLine("     {");
        txtstream.WriteLine("          border-style: ridge;");
        txtstream.WriteLine("     }");
        txtstream.WriteLine("     .inset");
        txtstream.WriteLine("     {");
        txtstream.WriteLine("          border-style: inset;");
        txtstream.WriteLine("     }");
        txtstream.WriteLine("     .groove");
        txtstream.WriteLine("     {");
        txtstream.WriteLine("          border-style: groove;");
        txtstream.WriteLine("     }");
        txtstream.WriteLine("     .dashed");
        txtstream.WriteLine("     {");
        txtstream.WriteLine("          border-style: dashed;");
        txtstream.WriteLine("     }");
        txtstream.WriteLine("     .dotted");
        txtstream.WriteLine("     {");
        txtstream.WriteLine("          border-style: dotted;");
        txtstream.WriteLine("     }");
        txtstream.WriteLine("     .outset");
        txtstream.WriteLine("     {");
        txtstream.WriteLine("          border-style: outset;");
        txtstream.WriteLine("     }");
```

```
                txtstream.WriteLine("          </style>");
                txtstream.WriteLine("     </head>");
                txtstream.WriteLine("     <body>");
        }
        public void Write_The_Table_To_HTML(string cnstr, string
tablename)
        {
                Array l;
                OleDbDataAdapter da = new OleDbDataAdapter("Select *
From " + tablename, cnstr);
                System.Data.DataTable dt = new
System.Data.DataTable();
                da.Fill(dt);

                int x = 0;
                l = Array.CreateInstance(typeof(int),
dt.Columns.Count);
                foreach (System.Data.DataColumn dc in dt.Columns)
                {
                    l.SetValue(dc.Caption.Length, x);
                    x = x + 1;
                }
                x = 0;
                foreach (System.Data.DataRow dr in dt.Rows)
                {
                    foreach (System.Data.DataColumn dc in dt.Columns)
                    {
                        int z = (int)l.GetValue(x);

                        if (z < dr[dc.Caption].ToString().Length)
                        {
l.SetValue(dr[dc.Caption].ToString().Length, x);
                        }
                        x = x + 1;
                    }
                    x = 0;
                }
                txtstream.WriteLine("                <table class =
\"table.main double\" frame=\"both\" rules=\"all\"
cellpadding=\"3px\" width=100%>");
                txtstream.WriteLine("                    <tr>");

                foreach(System.Data.DataColumn dc in dt.Columns)
                {
```

```
int z = (int)l.GetValue(x);
if (z == 0)
{
    z = 20;
}
else
{
    if (z < 10)
    {
        z = z * 8;
    }
    else
    {
        if (z < 30)
        {
            z = z * 7;
        }
        else
        {
            if (z < 50)
            {
                z = z * 6;
            }
            else
            {
                if (z < 70)
                {
                    z = z * 5;
                }
                else
                {
                    if (z < 90)
                    {
                        z = z * (int)4.5;
                    }
                    else
                    {
                        z = (z - 100) * 4;
                    }
                }
            }
        }
    }
}
```

```
            txtstream.WriteLine("                                <th
style=\"width:" + z + "px\">" + dc.Caption + "</th>");
            z = 0;
            x = x + 1;
        }
        x = 0;
        txtstream.WriteLine("                          </tr>");

        foreach(System.Data.DataRow dr in dt.Rows)
        {
            txtstream.WriteLine("                    <tr>");
            foreach(System.Data.DataColumn dc in dt.Columns)
            {
                int z = (int)l.GetValue(x);
                if (z == 0)
                {
                    z = 20;
                }
                else
                {
                    if (z < 10)
                    {
                        z = z * 8;
                    }
                    else
                    {
                        if (z < 30)
                        {
                            z = z * 7;
                        }
                        else
                        {
                            if (z < 50)
                            {
                                z = z * 6;
                            }
                            else
                            {
                                if (z < 90)
                                {
                                    z = z * 5;
                                }
                                else
                                {
                                    if (z < 200)
```

```
                                    {
                                        z = z * (int)4;
                                    }
                                    else
                                    {
                                        z = (z - 400) * 4;
                                    }
                                }
                            }
                        }
                    }
                }
                try
                {
                    txtstream.WriteLine("
<td><input type='text' Value='" + dr[dc.Caption].ToString() + "'
style=\"width:" + z + "px\"></input></td>");
                }
                catch (Exception ex)
                {
                    txtstream.WriteLine("
<td><input type='text' style=\"width:" + z +
"px\"></input></td>");
                }
                z = 0;
                x = x + 1;
            }
            txtstream.WriteLine("                              </tr>");
            x = 0;
        }
        txtstream.WriteLine("                    </tbody>");
        txtstream.WriteLine("            </table>");
    }
    public void End_The_Show()
    {
        txtstream.WriteLine("        </body>");
        txtstream.WriteLine("</html>");
        txtstream.Close();
    }
    }
}
```

And the results:

AcceptPause	AcceptStop	Caption	CheckPoint	CreationClassName	DelayedAutoStart	Description
FALSE	TRUE	System Event Notification Service	0	Win32_Service	FALSE	Monitors system events and notifies subscribers to COM+ Event System of these events.
FALSE	FALSE	Sensor Data Service	0	Win32_Service	FALSE	Delivers data from a variety of sensors
FALSE	FALSE	Sensor Service	0	Win32_Service	FALSE	A service for sensors that manages different sensors
FALSE	FALSE	Sensor Monitoring Service	0	Win32_Service	FALSE	Monitors various sensors in order to expose data and adapt to system and user state. If thi
FALSE	FALSE	Remote Desktop Configuration	0	Win32_Service	FALSE	Remote Desktop Configuration service (RDCS) is responsible for all Remote Desktop Servi
FALSE	FALSE	Internet Connection Sharing (ICS)	0	Win32_Service	FALSE	Provides network address translation, addressing, name resolution and/or intrusion pre
FALSE	TRUE	Shell Hardware Detection	0	Win32_Service	FALSE	Provides notifications for AutoPlay hardware events.
FALSE	FALSE	Microsoft Storage Spaces SMP	0	Win32_Service	FALSE	Host service for the Microsoft Storage Spaces management provider. If this service is stopp
FALSE	FALSE	SNMP Trap	0	Win32_Service	FALSE	Receives trap messages generated by local or remote Simple Network Management Protoc
FALSE	TRUE	Print Spooler	0	Win32_Service	FALSE	This service spools print jobs and handles interaction with the printer. If you turn off this
FALSE	FALSE	Software Protection	0	Win32_Service	TRUE	Enables the download, installation and enforcement of digital licenses for Windows and
FALSE	FALSE	SQL Server Agent (SQLEXPRESS)	0	Win32_Service	FALSE	Executes jobs, monitors SQL Server, fires alerts, and allows automation of some administr
FALSE	FALSE	SQL Server Browser	0	Win32_Service	FALSE	Provides SQL Server connection information to client computers.
FALSE	TRUE	SQL Server VSS Writer	0	Win32_Service	FALSE	Provides the interface to backup/restore Microsoft SQL server through the Windows VSS i
FALSE	TRUE	SSDP Discovery	0	Win32_Service	FALSE	Discovers networked devices and services that use the SSDP discovery protocol, such as U
FALSE	FALSE	Secure Socket Tunneling Protocol Service	0	Win32_Service	FALSE	Provides support for the Secure Socket Tunneling Protocol (SSTP) to connect to remote co
FALSE	TRUE	State Repository Service	0	Win32_Service	FALSE	Provides required infrastructure support for the application model.
TRUE	TRUE	Windows Image Acquisition (WIA)	0	Win32_Service	FALSE	Provides image acquisition services for scanners and cameras.

As I said, the fine tuning of the widths is roughed in but close enough to make the webpage and all of the input boxes look a heck of a lot better than what was being tried that didn't work.

Below, is the code that drives the class:

```
using System;
using System.Collections.Generic;
using System.ComponentModel;
using System.Data;
using System.Drawing;
using System.Linq;
using System.Text;
using System.Windows.Forms;
using System.Management;
using System.Security;
using ADOX;
using ADODB;


namespace WindowsFormsApplication1
{
    public partial class Form1 : Form
    {
        public Form1()
        {
            InitializeComponent();
        }
```

```
        private void Form1_Load(object sender, EventArgs e)
        {

            Class1 mchammer = new Class1();
            string tempstr = System.Environment.CurrentDirectory
+ "\\test.html";
            mchammer.Start_The_Show(tempstr, "properties");

mchammer.Write_The_Table_To_HTML("Provider=Microsoft.Jet.Oledb.4.
0;Data Source=" + System.Environment.CurrentDirectory +
"\\service.mdb", "Properties");
            mchammer.End_The_Show();
            webBrowser1.Navigate(tempstr);


        }
    }
}
```

Expanding the possibilities

Because ASP, ASPX and HTA code so close to straight HTML, I've decided to add their routines to this book. Simply put, if you code up to do one, you might as well get acquainted with just how easy it is to code up the other three.

HTA

Here's an example of using HTA or Hypertext Application which will use an older browser. Meaning the browser will see align=left nowrap and all will be good.

Below is the code:

```
using System;
using System.Collections.Generic;
using System.Linq;
using System.Text;
using Scripting;
using System.Data;
using System.Data.OleDb;
namespace WindowsFormsApplication1
{
    class Class1
    {
```

```
        TextStream txtstream;
        public void Start_The_Show(string fName, string
tablename)
        {
            FileSystemObject fso = new FileSystemObject();
            txtstream = fso.OpenTextFile(fName,
IOMode.ForWriting, true, Tristate.TristateUseDefault);
            txtstream.WriteLine("<html>");
            txtstream.WriteLine("    <head>");
            txtstream.WriteLine("<HTA:APPLICATION ");
            txtstream.WriteLine("NAVIGABLE = 'no' ");
            txtstream.WriteLine("ID = '" + tablename + "' ");
            txtstream.WriteLine("APPLICATIONNAME = '" + tablename
+ "' ");
            txtstream.WriteLine("SCROLL = 'no' ");
            txtstream.WriteLine("BorderStyle = 'normal' ");
            txtstream.WriteLine("SINGLEINSTANCE = 'yes' ");
            txtstream.WriteLine("WINDOWSTATE = 'maximize' ");
            txtstream.WriteLine("BORDER = 'thin' ");
            txtstream.WriteLine("CAPTION = 'yes' ");
            txtstream.WriteLine("MAXIMIZEBUTTON = 'no' ");
            txtstream.WriteLine("MINIMIZEBUTTON = 'no' ");
            txtstream.WriteLine("SHOWINTASKBAR = 'no'");
            txtstream.WriteLine("SYSMENU = 'yes'");
            txtstream.WriteLine(">");
            txtstream.WriteLine("           <title>First
Page</title>");
            txtstream.WriteLine("           <style>");
            txtstream.WriteLine("           th");
            txtstream.WriteLine("           {");
            txtstream.WriteLine("              COLOR: white;");
            txtstream.WriteLine("              BACKGROUND-COLOR:
navy;");
            txtstream.WriteLine("              Font-family: Cambria,
serif;");
            txtstream.WriteLine("              FONT-SIZE: 12px;");
            txtstream.WriteLine("              text-align: left;");
            txtstream.WriteLine("           }");
            txtstream.WriteLine("           table.main");
            txtstream.WriteLine("           {");
            txtstream.WriteLine("              border-color:
navy;");
            txtstream.WriteLine("              border-width: 2px;");
            txtstream.WriteLine("              text-align: left");
            txtstream.WriteLine("           }");
```

```
            txtstream.WriteLine("         span");
            txtstream.WriteLine("         {");
            txtstream.WriteLine("             COLOR: black;");
            txtstream.WriteLine("             BACKGROUND-COLOR:
white;");
            txtstream.WriteLine("             Font-family: Cambria,
serif;");
            txtstream.WriteLine("             FONT-SIZE: 10px;");
            txtstream.WriteLine("         }");
            txtstream.WriteLine("         .solid");
            txtstream.WriteLine("         {");
            txtstream.WriteLine("             width: 100%;");
            txtstream.WriteLine("             display: inline-
block;");
            txtstream.WriteLine("         }");
            txtstream.WriteLine("         .double");
            txtstream.WriteLine("         {");
            txtstream.WriteLine("             border-style:
double;");
            txtstream.WriteLine("         }");
            txtstream.WriteLine("         .ridge");
            txtstream.WriteLine("         {");
            txtstream.WriteLine("             border-style:
ridge;");
            txtstream.WriteLine("         }");
            txtstream.WriteLine("         .inset");
            txtstream.WriteLine("         {");
            txtstream.WriteLine("             border-style:
inset;");
            txtstream.WriteLine("         }");
            txtstream.WriteLine("         .groove");
            txtstream.WriteLine("         {");
            txtstream.WriteLine("             border-style:
groove;");
            txtstream.WriteLine("         }");
            txtstream.WriteLine("         .dashed");
            txtstream.WriteLine("         {");
            txtstream.WriteLine("             border-style:
dashed;");
            txtstream.WriteLine("         }");
            txtstream.WriteLine("         .dotted");
            txtstream.WriteLine("         {");
            txtstream.WriteLine("             border-style:
dotted;");
            txtstream.WriteLine("         }");
```

```csharp
            txtstream.WriteLine("              .outset");
            txtstream.WriteLine("              {");
            txtstream.WriteLine("                  border-style:
outset;");
            txtstream.WriteLine("              }");
            txtstream.WriteLine("          </style>");
            txtstream.WriteLine("      </head>");
            txtstream.WriteLine("      <body>");
        }
        public void Write_The_Table_To_HTML(string cnstr, string
tablename)
        {

            OleDbDataAdapter da = new OleDbDataAdapter("Select *
From " + tablename, cnstr);
            System.Data.DataTable dt = new
System.Data.DataTable();
            da.Fill(dt);

            txtstream.WriteLine("          <table class =
\"table.main double\" frame=\"both\" rules=\"all\"
cellpadding=\"3px\" width=100%>");
            txtstream.WriteLine("              <thead>");
            txtstream.WriteLine("                  <tr>");
            foreach(System.Data.DataColumn dc in dt.Columns)
            {
                txtstream.WriteLine("                      <th>" +
dc.Caption + "</th>");
            }
            txtstream.WriteLine("                  </tr>");
            txtstream.WriteLine("              </thead>");
            txtstream.WriteLine("              <tbody>");
            foreach(System.Data.DataRow dr in dt.Rows)
            {
                txtstream.WriteLine("                  <tr>");
                foreach(System.Data.DataColumn dc in dt.Columns)
                {
                    try
                    {

                    txtstream.WriteLine("
<td align=left nowrap><span style=\"COLOR: black;BACKGROUND-
COLOR: white;Font-family: Cambria, serif;FONT-SIZE: 10px;text-
align: left;display:inline-block;white-space:nowrap='nowrap';\">"
+ dr[dc.Caption].ToString() + "</span></td>");
```

```csharp
                    }
                    catch (Exception ex)
                    {
                        txtstream.WriteLine("
<td align=left nowrap><span style=\"COLOR: black;BACKGROUND-
COLOR: white;Font-family: Cambria, serif;FONT-SIZE: 10px;text-
align: left;display:inline-block;white-
space:nowrap='nowrap';\"></span></td>");
                    }

                }
                txtstream.WriteLine("                                    </tr>");
            }
            txtstream.WriteLine("                    </tbody>");
            txtstream.WriteLine("            </table>");
        }
        public void End_The_Show()
        {
            txtstream.WriteLine("        </body>");
            txtstream.WriteLine("</html>");
            txtstream.Close();
        }

    }
}
```

The code making the call to the class:

```csharp
using System.Collections.Generic;
using System.ComponentModel;
using System.Data;
using System.Drawing;
using System.Linq;
using System.Text;
using System.Windows.Forms;
using System.Management;
using System.Security;
using ADOX;
using ADODB;


namespace WindowsFormsApplication1
{
    public partial class Form1 : Form
    {
```

```
public Form1()
{
    InitializeComponent();
}

private void Form1_Load(object sender, EventArgs e)
{

    Class2 mchammer = new Class2();
    string tempstr = System.Environment.CurrentDirectory
+ "\\test.hta";
    mchammer.Start_The_Show(tempstr, "properties");

mchammer.Write_The_Table_To_HTML("Provider=Microsoft.Jet.Oledb.4.
0;Data Source=" + System.Environment.CurrentDirectory +
"\\service.mdb", "Properties");
    mchammer.End_The_Show();
    webBrowser1.Navigate(tempstr);

}

}
}
```

This is the same code we used in the html examples but this time, we simply added the html for the hta application and used the hta extension to the filename.

Here's the results:

AcceptPause	AcceptStop	Caption	CheckPoint	CreationClassName	DelayedAutoStart
FALSE	TRUE	System Event Notification Service	0	Win32_Service	FALSE
FALSE	FALSE	Sensor Data Service	0	Win32_Service	FALSE
FALSE	FALSE	Sensor Service	0	Win32_Service	FALSE
FALSE	FALSE	Sensor Monitoring Service	0	Win32_Service	FALSE
FALSE	FALSE	Remote Desktop Configuration	0	Win32_Service	FALSE
FALSE	FALSE	Internet Connection Sharing (ICS)	0	Win32_Service	FALSE
FALSE	TRUE	Shell Hardware Detection	0	Win32_Service	FALSE
FALSE	FALSE	Microsoft Storage Spaces SMP	0	Win32_Service	FALSE
FALSE	FALSE	SNMP Trap	0	Win32_Service	FALSE
FALSE	TRUE	Print Spooler	0	Win32_Service	FALSE
FALSE	FALSE	Software Protection	0	Win32_Service	TRUE
FALSE	FALSE	SQL Server Agent (SQLEXPRESS)	0	Win32_Service	FALSE
FALSE	FALSE	SQL Server Browser	0	Win32_Service	FALSE
FALSE	TRUE	SQL Server VSS Writer	0	Win32_Service	FALSE
FALSE	TRUE	SSDP Discovery	0	Win32_Service	FALSE
FALSE	FALSE	Secure Socket Tunneling Protocol Service	0	Win32_Service	FALSE
FALSE	TRUE	State Repository Service	0	Win32_Service	FALSE
TRUE	TRUE	Windows Image Acquisition (WIA)	0	Win32_Service	FALSE

ASP

Since we're pretty much doing the heavy lifting – so to speak – the same exact code used in the example for ASPX can be used to create an ASP page. Simply put, we aren't doing anything fancy here. We're just taking the html and saving it as an asp webpage.

So, this is the code that runs and creates the asp page:

```
using System;
using System.Collections.Generic;
using System.Linq;
using System.Text;
using System.Data;
using System.Data.OleDb;
using Scripting;


namespace WindowsFormsApplication1
{
    class Class3
    {
        TextStream txtstream;
```

```csharp
public void Start_The_Show(string fName, string
tablename)
    {
        FileSystemObject fso = new FileSystemObject();
        txtstream = fso.OpenTextFile(fName,
IOMode.ForWriting, true, Tristate.TristateUseDefault);
        txtstream.WriteLine("<html>");
        txtstream.WriteLine("    <head>");
        txtstream.WriteLine("
<title>ASPPage</title>");
        txtstream.WriteLine("            <style>");
        txtstream.WriteLine("            th");
        txtstream.WriteLine("            {");
        txtstream.WriteLine("                COLOR: white;");
        txtstream.WriteLine("                BACKGROUND-COLOR:
navy;");
        txtstream.WriteLine("                Font-family: Cambria,
serif;");
        txtstream.WriteLine("                FONT-SIZE: 12px;");
        txtstream.WriteLine("                text-align: left;");
        txtstream.WriteLine("                display:table-
cell;");
        txtstream.WriteLine("                white-Space:
nowrap;");
        txtstream.WriteLine("            }");
        txtstream.WriteLine("            td");
        txtstream.WriteLine("            {");
        txtstream.WriteLine("                color: black;");
        txtstream.WriteLine("                background-color:
white;");
        txtstream.WriteLine("                font-size:10px;");
        txtstream.WriteLine("                font-family:Calibri,
Sans-Serif;");
        txtstream.WriteLine("                display:table-
cell;");
        txtstream.WriteLine("                text-align: left");
        txtstream.WriteLine("                white-space:
nowrap;");
        txtstream.WriteLine("            }");
        txtstream.WriteLine("            table.main");
        txtstream.WriteLine("            {");
        txtstream.WriteLine("                border-color:
navy;");
        txtstream.WriteLine("                border-width: 2px;");
        txtstream.WriteLine("                text-align: left");
```

```
txtstream.WriteLine("          }");
txtstream.WriteLine("          input");
txtstream.WriteLine("          {");
txtstream.WriteLine("              COLOR: black;");
txtstream.WriteLine("              BACKGROUND-COLOR: white;");
txtstream.WriteLine("              Font-family: Cambria, serif;");
txtstream.WriteLine("              FONT-SIZE: 10px;");
txtstream.WriteLine("              text-align: left");
txtstream.WriteLine("              white-Space: nowrap;");
txtstream.WriteLine("              width:100%;");
txtstream.WriteLine("          }");
txtstream.WriteLine("          .solid");
txtstream.WriteLine("          {");
txtstream.WriteLine("              width: 100%;");
txtstream.WriteLine("              display: inline-block;");
txtstream.WriteLine("          }");
txtstream.WriteLine("          .double");
txtstream.WriteLine("          {");
txtstream.WriteLine("              border-style: double;");
txtstream.WriteLine("          }");
txtstream.WriteLine("          .ridge");
txtstream.WriteLine("          {");
txtstream.WriteLine("              border-style: ridge;");
txtstream.WriteLine("          }");
txtstream.WriteLine("          .inset");
txtstream.WriteLine("          {");
txtstream.WriteLine("              border-style: inset;");
txtstream.WriteLine("          }");
txtstream.WriteLine("          .groove");
txtstream.WriteLine("          {");
txtstream.WriteLine("              border-style: groove;");
txtstream.WriteLine("          }");
txtstream.WriteLine("          .dashed");
txtstream.WriteLine("          {");
txtstream.WriteLine("              border-style: dashed;");
txtstream.WriteLine("          }");
```

```
            txtstream.WriteLine("        .dotted");
            txtstream.WriteLine("        {");
            txtstream.WriteLine("            border-style:
dotted;");
            txtstream.WriteLine("        }");
            txtstream.WriteLine("        .outset");
            txtstream.WriteLine("        {");
            txtstream.WriteLine("            border-style:
outset;");
            txtstream.WriteLine("        }");
            txtstream.WriteLine("        </style>");
            txtstream.WriteLine("    </head>");
            txtstream.WriteLine("    <body>");
        }
        public void Write_The_Table_To_HTML(string cnstr, string
tablename)
        {
            Array l;
            OleDbDataAdapter da = new OleDbDataAdapter("Select *
From " + tablename, cnstr);
            System.Data.DataTable dt = new
System.Data.DataTable();
            da.Fill(dt);

            int x = 0;
            l = Array.CreateInstance(typeof(int),
dt.Columns.Count);
            foreach (System.Data.DataColumn dc in dt.Columns)
            {
                l.SetValue(dc.Caption.Length, x);
                x = x + 1;
            }
            x = 0;
            foreach (System.Data.DataRow dr in dt.Rows)
            {
                foreach (System.Data.DataColumn dc in dt.Columns)
                {
                    int z = (int)l.GetValue(x);

                    if (z < dr[dc.Caption].ToString().Length)
                    {
l.SetValue(dr[dc.Caption].ToString().Length, x);
                    }
                    x = x + 1;
```

```
            }
            x = 0;
        }
        txtstream.WriteLine("            <table class =
\"table.main double\" frame=\"both\" rules=\"all\"
cellpadding=\"3px\" width=100%>");
        txtstream.WriteLine("                <tr>");

        foreach (System.Data.DataColumn dc in dt.Columns)
        {
            int z = (int)l.GetValue(x);
            if (z == 0)
            {
                z = 20;
            }
            else
            {
                if (z < 10)
                {
                    z = z * 8;
                }
                else
                {
                    if (z < 30)
                    {
                        z = z * 7;
                    }
                    else
                    {
                        if (z < 50)
                        {
                            z = z * 6;
                        }
                        else
                        {
                            if (z < 70)
                            {
                                z = z * 5;
                            }
                            else
                            {
                                if (z < 90)
                                {
                                    z = z * (int)4.5;
                                }
```

```
                            else
                            {
                                z = (z - 100) * 4;
                            }
                        }
                    }
                }
            }
        }

        txtstream.WriteLine("                    <th
style=\"width:" + z + "px\">" + dc.Caption + "</th>");
            z = 0;
            x = x + 1;
        }
        x = 0;
        txtstream.WriteLine("                    </tr>");

        foreach (System.Data.DataRow dr in dt.Rows)
        {
            txtstream.WriteLine("                    <tr>");
            foreach (System.Data.DataColumn dc in dt.Columns)
            {
                int z = (int)l.GetValue(x);
                if (z == 0)
                {
                    z = 20;
                }
                else
                {
                    if (z < 10)
                    {
                        z = z * 8;
                    }
                    else
                    {
                        if (z < 30)
                        {
                            z = z * 7;
                        }
                        else
                        {
                            if (z < 50)
                            {
                                z = z * 6;
```

```csharp
                        }
                        else
                        {
                            if (z < 90)
                            {
                                z = z * 5;
                            }
                            else
                            {
                                if (z < 200)
                                {
                                    z = z * (int)4;
                                }
                                else
                                {
                                    z = (z - 400) * 4;
                                }
                            }
                        }
                    }
                }
            }
            try
            {
                txtstream.WriteLine("
<td><input type='text' Value='" + dr[dc.Caption].ToString() + "'
style=\"width:" + z + "px\"></input></td>");
            }
            catch (Exception ex)
            {
                txtstream.WriteLine("
<td><input type='text' style=\"width:" + z +
"px\"></input></td>");
            }
            z = 0;
            x = x + 1;
        }
        txtstream.WriteLine("                        </tr>");
        x = 0;
    }
    txtstream.WriteLine("            </tbody>");
    txtstream.WriteLine("        </table>");
}
public void End_The_Show()
{
```

```
            txtstream.WriteLine("     </body>");
            txtstream.WriteLine("</html>");
            txtstream.Close();
        }
    }
}
```

Here's the results:

AcceptPause	AcceptStop	Caption	CheckPoint	CreationClassName	DelayedAutoStart	Description
FALSE	TRUE	System Event Notification Service	0	Win32_Service	FALSE	Monitors system
FALSE	FALSE	Sensor Data Service	0	Win32_Service	FALSE	Delivers data fro
FALSE	FALSE	Sensor Service	0	Win32_Service	FALSE	A service for sen
FALSE	FALSE	Sensor Monitoring Service	0	Win32_Service	FALSE	Monitors variou
FALSE	FALSE	Remote Desktop Configuration	0	Win32_Service	FALSE	Remote Desktop
FALSE	FALSE	Internet Connection Sharing (ICS)	0	Win32_Service	FALSE	Provides networ
FALSE	TRUE	Shell Hardware Detection	0	Win32_Service	FALSE	Provides notific
FALSE	FALSE	Microsoft Storage Spaces SMP	0	Win32_Service	FALSE	Host service for
FALSE	FALSE	SNMP Trap	0	Win32_Service	FALSE	Receives trap me
FALSE	TRUE	Print Spooler	0	Win32_Service	FALSE	This service spo
FALSE	FALSE	Software Protection	0	Win32_Service	TRUE	Enables the dow
FALSE	FALSE	SQL Server Agent (SQLEXPRESS)	0	Win32_Service	FALSE	Executes jobs. m
FALSE	FALSE	SQL Server Browser	0	Win32_Service	FALSE	Provides SQL Se
FALSE	TRUE	SQL Server VSS Writer	0	Win32_Service	FALSE	Provides the inti
FALSE	TRUE	SSDP Discovery	0	Win32_Service	FALSE	Discovers netwo

After creating the code, all I did was open the asp file in notepad, highlight the file contents and copy the contents into notepad. Then added a new webform and deleted the contents inside the form – leaving nothing to the imagination, pasted the HTML directly into the empty webform.

The results above were in the browser after the web application was started in debug mode.

ASPX

The first thing you're going to notice is the fact that we are creating aspx code. That might sound trite and obvious, but the fact is, you can't use the same code – as we did with the asp page – as a straight html page. The browser doesn't know what to do with those tags!

With that said, here's the code:

```
using System;
using System.Collections.Generic;
using System.Linq;
using System.Text;
using Scripting;
using System.Data;
using System.Data.OleDb;

namespace WindowsFormsApplication1
{
    class ClassASPX
    {

        TextStream txtstream;
        public void Start_The_Show(string fName, string tablename)
        {
            FileSystemObject fso = new FileSystemObject();
            txtstream = fso.OpenTextFile(fName,
IOMode.ForWriting, true, Tristate.TristateUseDefault);
            txtstream.WriteLine("<html
xmlns=\"http://www.w3.org/1999/xhtml\">");
            txtstream.WriteLine("<head runat=\"server\">");
            txtstream.WriteLine("<title>" + tablename +
"</title>");
            txtstream.WriteLine("<style runat=\"server\">");
            txtstream.WriteLine("th");
            txtstream.WriteLine("{");
            txtstream.WriteLine("    COLOR: white;");
            txtstream.WriteLine("    BACKGROUND-COLOR: navy;");
            txtstream.WriteLine("    Font-family: Cambria,
serif;");
            txtstream.WriteLine("    FONT-SIZE: 12px;");
            txtstream.WriteLine("    text-align: left;");
            txtstream.WriteLine("    display:table-cell;");
            txtstream.WriteLine("    white-Space:
nowrap='nowrap';");
            txtstream.WriteLine("    width:auto;");
            txtstream.WriteLine("}");
```

```
txtstream.WriteLine("td");
txtstream.WriteLine("{");
txtstream.WriteLine("    color: black;");
txtstream.WriteLine("    background-color: white;");
txtstream.WriteLine("    font-size:10px;");
txtstream.WriteLine("    font-family:Calibri, Sans-
Serif;");
txtstream.WriteLine("    display:table-cell;");
txtstream.WriteLine("    white-space:
nowrap='nowrap';");
txtstream.WriteLine("    width:auto;");
txtstream.WriteLine("}");
txtstream.WriteLine("table.main");
txtstream.WriteLine("{");
txtstream.WriteLine("    border-color: navy;");
txtstream.WriteLine("    border-width: 2px;");
txtstream.WriteLine("    text-align: left");
txtstream.WriteLine("}");
txtstream.WriteLine("span");
txtstream.WriteLine("{");
txtstream.WriteLine("    COLOR: black;");
txtstream.WriteLine("    BACKGROUND-COLOR: white;");
txtstream.WriteLine("    Font-family: Cambria,
serif;");
txtstream.WriteLine("    FONT-SIZE: 10px;");
txtstream.WriteLine("}");
txtstream.WriteLine(".solid");
txtstream.WriteLine("{");
txtstream.WriteLine("    width: 100%;");
txtstream.WriteLine("    display: inline-block;");
txtstream.WriteLine("}");
txtstream.WriteLine(".double");
txtstream.WriteLine("{");
txtstream.WriteLine("    border-style: double;");
txtstream.WriteLine("}");
txtstream.WriteLine(".ridge");
txtstream.WriteLine("{");
txtstream.WriteLine("    border-style: ridge;");
txtstream.WriteLine("}");
txtstream.WriteLine(".inset");
txtstream.WriteLine("{");
txtstream.WriteLine("    border-style: inset;");
txtstream.WriteLine("}");
txtstream.WriteLine(".groove");
txtstream.WriteLine("{");
```

```
            txtstream.WriteLine("    border-style: groove;");
            txtstream.WriteLine("}");
            txtstream.WriteLine(".dashed");
            txtstream.WriteLine("{");
            txtstream.WriteLine("    border-style: dashed;");
            txtstream.WriteLine("}");
            txtstream.WriteLine(".dotted");
            txtstream.WriteLine("{");
            txtstream.WriteLine("    border-style: dotted;");
            txtstream.WriteLine("}");
            txtstream.WriteLine(".outset");
            txtstream.WriteLine("{");
            txtstream.WriteLine("    border-style: outset;");
            txtstream.WriteLine("}");
            txtstream.WriteLine("</style>");
            txtstream.WriteLine("    </head>");
            txtstream.WriteLine("    <body>");
            txtstream.WriteLine("        <form id=\"form1\"
runat=\"server\">");
            txtstream.WriteLine("            <div>");
            txtstream.WriteLine("            <asp:Table
runat=\"server\">");
        }

    public void Write_The_Table_To_HTML(string cnstr, string
tablename)
        {

            OleDbDataAdapter da = new OleDbDataAdapter("Select *
From " + tablename, cnstr);
            System.Data.DataTable dt = new
System.Data.DataTable();
            da.Fill(dt);

            txtstream.WriteLine("            <table CSSClass =
\"table.main double\">");
            txtstream.WriteLine("
<asp:TableHeaderRow>");
            foreach (System.Data.DataColumn dc in dt.Columns)
            {
                txtstream.WriteLine("
<asp:TableHeaderCell>" + dc.Caption + "</asp:TableHeaderCell>");
            }
            txtstream.WriteLine("
</asp:TableHeaderRow>");
```

```csharp
                foreach (System.Data.DataRow dr in dt.Rows)
                {
                    txtstream.WriteLine("
<asp:TableRow>");
                        foreach (System.Data.DataColumn dc in dt.Columns)
                        {
                            try
                            {

                                txtstream.WriteLine("
<asp:Tablecell runat=\"server\"><span>" +
dr[dc.Caption].ToString() + "</span></asp:Tablecell>");
                            }
                            catch (Exception ex)
                            {
                                txtstream.WriteLine("
<asp:Tablecell runat=\"server\"><span></span></asp:Tablecell>");
                            }

                        }
                    txtstream.WriteLine("
</asp:TableRow>");
                }

        }
        public void End_The_Show()
        {
            txtstream.WriteLine("                        </asp:Table>");
            txtstream.WriteLine("                    </div>");
            txtstream.WriteLine("                </form>");
            txtstream.WriteLine("        </body>");
            txtstream.WriteLine("</html>");
            txtstream.Close();
        }

    }
}
```

And the code to run the class:

```csharp
using System;
using System.Collections.Generic;
```

```csharp
using System.ComponentModel;
using System.Data;
using System.Drawing;
using System.Linq;
using System.Text;
using System.Windows.Forms;
using System.Management;
using System.Security;
using ADOX;
using ADODB;


namespace WindowsFormsApplication1
{
    public partial class Form1 : Form
    {
        public Form1()
        {
            InitializeComponent();
        }

        private void Form1_Load(object sender, EventArgs e)
        {

            //do_Initialization_Code();
            ClassASPX mchammer = new ClassASPX();
            string tempstr = System.Environment.CurrentDirectory
+ "\\test.aspx";
            mchammer.Start_The_Show(tempstr, "properties");

mchammer.Write_The_Table_To_HTML("Provider=Microsoft.Jet.Oledb.4.
0;Data Source=" + System.Environment.CurrentDirectory +
"\\service.mdb", "Properties");
            mchammer.End_The_Show();
            webBrowser1.Navigate(tempstr);
        }

    }

}
```

The output from this routine looks like this:

```
<html xmlns="http://www.w3.org/1999/xhtml">
```

```html
<head id="Head1" runat="server">
<title>properties</title>
<style id="Style1" runat="server">
th
{
    COLOR: white;
    BACKGROUND-COLOR: navy;
    Font-family: Cambria, serif;
    FONT-SIZE: 12px;
    text-align: left;
    display:table-cell;
    white-Space: nowrap='nowrap';
    width:auto;
}
td
{
    color: black;
    background-color: white;
    font-size:10px;
    font-family:Calibri, Sans-Serif;
    display:table-cell;
    white-space: nowrap;
    width:auto;
}
table.main
{
    border-color: navy;
    border-width: 2px;
    text-align: left;
    white-space: nowrap;
}
span
{
    COLOR: black;
    BACKGROUND-COLOR: white;
    Font-family: Cambria, serif;
    FONT-SIZE: 10px;
    text-align:left;
    white-space: nowrap;

}
.solid
{
    width: 100%;
    display: inline-block;
```

```
}
.double
{
    border-style: double;
}
.ridge
{
    border-style: ridge;
}
.inset
{
    border-style: inset;
}
.groove
{
    border-style: groove;
}
.dashed
{
    border-style: dashed;
}
.dotted
{
    border-style: dotted;
}
.outset
{
    border-style: outset;
}
</style>
    </head>
    <body>
        <form id="form1" runat="server">
            <div>
                <asp:Table ID="Table1" runat="server" CssClass =
"table.main double">
                    <asp:TableHeaderRow>

<asp:TableHeaderCell>AcceptPause</asp:TableHeaderCell>

<asp:TableHeaderCell>AcceptStop</asp:TableHeaderCell>

<asp:TableHeaderCell>Caption</asp:TableHeaderCell>

<asp:TableHeaderCell>CheckPoint</asp:TableHeaderCell>
```

```
<asp:TableHeaderCell>CreationClassName</asp:TableHeaderCell>

<asp:TableHeaderCell>DelayedAutoStart</asp:TableHeaderCell>

<asp:TableHeaderCell>Description</asp:TableHeaderCell>

<asp:TableHeaderCell>DesktopInteract</asp:TableHeaderCell>

<asp:TableHeaderCell>DisplayName</asp:TableHeaderCell>

<asp:TableHeaderCell>ErrorControl</asp:TableHeaderCell>

<asp:TableHeaderCell>ExitCode</asp:TableHeaderCell>

<asp:TableHeaderCell>InstallDate</asp:TableHeaderCell>

<asp:TableHeaderCell>Name</asp:TableHeaderCell>

<asp:TableHeaderCell>PathName</asp:TableHeaderCell>

<asp:TableHeaderCell>ProcessId</asp:TableHeaderCell>

<asp:TableHeaderCell>ServiceSpecificExitCode</asp:TableHeaderCell>

<asp:TableHeaderCell>ServiceType</asp:TableHeaderCell>

<asp:TableHeaderCell>Started</asp:TableHeaderCell>

<asp:TableHeaderCell>StartMode</asp:TableHeaderCell>

<asp:TableHeaderCell>StartName</asp:TableHeaderCell>

<asp:TableHeaderCell>State</asp:TableHeaderCell>

<asp:TableHeaderCell>Status</asp:TableHeaderCell>

<asp:TableHeaderCell>SystemCreationClassName</asp:TableHeaderCell>

<asp:TableHeaderCell>SystemName</asp:TableHeaderCell>

<asp:TableHeaderCell>TagId</asp:TableHeaderCell>
```

```
<asp:TableHeaderCell>WaitHint</asp:TableHeaderCell>
                        </asp:TableHeaderRow>
                        <asp:TableRow>
                              <asp:Tablecell ID="Tablecell1"
runat="server"><span>FALSE</span></asp:Tablecell>
                              <asp:Tablecell ID="Tablecell2"
runat="server"><span>TRUE</span></asp:Tablecell>
                              <asp:Tablecell ID="Tablecell3"
runat="server"><span>System Event Notification
Service</span></asp:Tablecell>
                              <asp:Tablecell ID="Tablecell4"
runat="server"><span>0</span></asp:Tablecell>
                              <asp:Tablecell ID="Tablecell5"
runat="server"><span>Win32_Service</span></asp:Tablecell>
                              <asp:Tablecell ID="Tablecell6"
runat="server"><span>FALSE</span></asp:Tablecell>
                              <asp:Tablecell ID="Tablecell7"
runat="server"><span>Monitors system events and notifies
subscribers to COM+ Event System of these
events.</span></asp:Tablecell>
                              <asp:Tablecell ID="Tablecell8"
runat="server"><span>FALSE</span></asp:Tablecell>
                              <asp:Tablecell ID="Tablecell9"
runat="server"><span>System Event Notification
Service</span></asp:Tablecell>
                              <asp:Tablecell ID="Tablecell10"
runat="server"><span>Normal</span></asp:Tablecell>
                              <asp:Tablecell ID="Tablecell11"
runat="server"><span>0</span></asp:Tablecell>
                              <asp:Tablecell ID="Tablecell12"
runat="server"><span></span></asp:Tablecell>
                              <asp:Tablecell ID="Tablecell13"
runat="server"><span>Win32_Service</span></asp:Tablecell>
                              <asp:Tablecell ID="Tablecell14"
runat="server"><span>C:\\Windows\\system32\\svchost.exe -k
netsvcs</span></asp:Tablecell>
                              <asp:Tablecell ID="Tablecell15"
runat="server"><span>1232</span></asp:Tablecell>
                              <asp:Tablecell ID="Tablecell16"
runat="server"><span>0</span></asp:Tablecell>
                              <asp:Tablecell ID="Tablecell17"
runat="server"><span>Share Process</span></asp:Tablecell>
                              <asp:Tablecell ID="Tablecell18"
runat="server"><span>TRUE</span></asp:Tablecell>
```

```
                    <asp:Tablecell ID="Tablecell119"
runat="server"><span>Auto</span></asp:Tablecell>
                    <asp:Tablecell ID="Tablecell120"
runat="server"><span>LocalSystem</span></asp:Tablecell>
                    <asp:Tablecell ID="Tablecell121"
runat="server"><span>Running</span></asp:Tablecell>
                    <asp:Tablecell ID="Tablecell122"
runat="server"><span>OK</span></asp:Tablecell>
                    <asp:Tablecell ID="Tablecell123"
runat="server"><span>Win32_ComputerSystem</span></asp:Tablecell>
                    <asp:Tablecell ID="Tablecell124"
runat="server"><span>WIN-EPAKQO82F29</span></asp:Tablecell>
                    <asp:Tablecell ID="Tablecell125"
runat="server"><span>0</span></asp:Tablecell>
                    <asp:Tablecell ID="Tablecell126"
runat="server"><span>0</span></asp:Tablecell>
                </asp:TableRow>
            </asp:Table>
        </div>
      </form>
   </body>
</html>
```

The output looks like this:

So, I initially did this using Visual Studio 2010. The logic behind that decision was since it was an older version of Visual Studio, the CSS - white-space: nowrap; - should work perfectly fine. And, of course it did.

But Visual Studio 2010 is old. So, I wanted to see if the partial code I used above would work in Visual Studio 2019.

Except for the fact that Visual Studio 2019 complained about not having semi-colons at the end of some of the stylesheet setting – which I fixed – it also rendered the page just the way I wanted it.

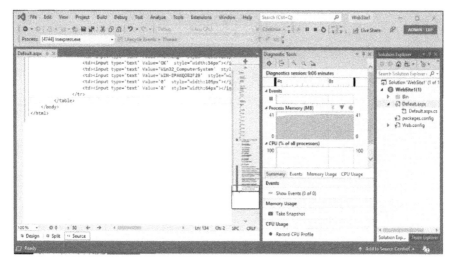

The proof:

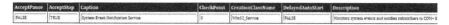

AcceptPause	AcceptStop	Caption	CheckPoint	CreationClassName	DelayedAutoStart	Description
FALSE	TRUE	System Event Notification Service	0	Win32_Service	FALSE	Monitors system events and notifies subscribers to COM+ E

Now, its time to do some stuff with SQL Server.

DRIVING YOUR WEBPAGES WITH SQL SERVER

A crash course with as simple as it can get air bags

Okay, you are about to learn a few things about SQL Server and be able to connect to SQL Server, create a database and table. Once created, we're going populate it with information and then take what we've already created using the same Access Database code.

That's about as simple and straight forward as I can get.

There are two things to remember which will make this just about as easy as flipping a switch. First, the connection string used to connect to SQL Server is different that the one used with Access.

In Access, we created a connection string that looked like this:

"Provider=Microsoft.Jet.Oledb.4.0;Data   Source="   +
System.Environment.CurrentDirectory + "\\" + databasename + ".mdb"

What this connection string is basically saying is: I want to use the Microsoft Jet OLEDB 4.0 provider, my database is in the same folder as my running program, its name is something I made up on the fly and the file extension is mdb.

For SQL Server, the connection string looks like this:

"Provider=SQLOLEDB;Data   Source=.;Integrated   Security=sspi;Initial   Catalog
=Processes"

What we're saying here is we want to use the Microsoft Provider for SQL Server – the SQLOLEDB, SQL Server is located on this machine. We don't want to pass in the username or password so where using integrated security and the database – the Initial Catalog - is Processes.

Now, if I didn't want to use Integrated Security and a UserName and Password instead, I would drop the Integrated Security=SSPI and add: User Id=;Password=; and add my username and password to those properties.

Right now, we just want to connect to SQL Server and create our database.

So, after installing SQL Server – I download SQL Server 2019 – and installed it. The download by the way wasn't smooth. There were about 6 retries to finally have the ISO on my machine.

I just went with the defaults and added the current user to all the prompts and grabbed myself a cup of coffee and waited for the install to finish.

At this point, I wrote the following code:

```
ADODB.Connection cn = new ADODB.Connection();
    cn.ConnectionString = "Provider=SQLOLEDB;Data Source=.;Integrated
Security=SSPI;";
    cn.Open();
    Object myobj = new Object();
    cn.Execute("CREATE DATABASE Processes", out myobj);
```

This worked to create the database. How did I know it worked? I went over to C:\Program Files\Microsoft SQL Server\MSSQL15.MSSQLSERVER\MSSQL\DATA and found this:

Processes	12/4/2019 12:17 PM	SQL Server Databa...	8,192 KB
Processes_log	12/4/2019 12:17 PM	SQL Server Databa...	8,192 KB

After this, I wanted to create the table and populate it with Win32_Process information.

ADODB.Connection cn = new ADODB.Connection();

```csharp
        cn.ConnectionString = "Provider=SQLOLEDB;Data Source=.;Integrated
Security=SSPI; Initial Catalog=Processes";
        cn.Open();

        string tempstr = "CREATE TABLE ProcessProperties(";

        ConnectionOptions cops = new ConnectionOptions();
        cops.Authentication = AuthenticationLevel.PacketPrivacy;
        cops.Impersonation = ImpersonationLevel.Impersonate;
        cops.Locale = "MS0409";

        ManagementPath path = new ManagementPath();
        path.ClassName = "Win32_Process";
        path.NamespacePath = "root\\cimv2";
        path.Server = "LocalHost";

        ManagementScope scope = new ManagementScope(path, cops);
        scope.Connect();

        ManagementObjectSearcher mos = new ManagementObjectSearcher();
        mos.Scope.Path = scope.Path;
        mos.Query.QueryString = "Select * From Win32_Process";
        ManagementObjectCollection moc = mos.Get();
        ManagementObjectCollection.ManagementObjectEnumerator    mocEnum    =
moc.GetEnumerator();
        while (mocEnum.MoveNext())
        {
            ManagementBaseObject mo = mocEnum.Current;
            PropertyDataCollection props = mo.Properties;
            String tstr = "";
            foreach (PropertyData prop in props)
            {
                if (tstr != "")
```

```
        {
            tstr = tstr + ", ";
        }
        tstr = tstr + prop.Name + " text";
    }
    tempstr = tempstr + tstr + ")";

    Object myobj = new object();
    cn.Execute(tempstr, out myobj);
    break;
}
```

At this point, we now have a SQL Database and Table with empty fields just waiting to get populated.

By the way, the text datatype was used for simplicity and ease of use. I could have tried to marry up the WMI datatypes to their SQL versions, but that would take a lot more time to do and, quite simply, I wanted to just create the table with what I know works.

Now, I had to populate the table:

```
        mocEnum.Reset();
        Populate_The_Table(mocEnum);

    }
    private void
Populate_The_Table(ManagementObjectCollection.ManagementObjectEnu
merator mocEnum)
    {

        ADODB.Recordset rs = new ADODB.Recordset();
        rs.let_ActiveConnection("Provider=SQLOLEDB;Data
Source=.;Integrated Security=SSPI;Initial Catalog=Processes");
        rs.LockType = LockTypeEnum.adLockPessimistic;
        rs.CursorLocation = CursorLocationEnum.adUseClient;
        rs.let_Source("Select * From ProcessProperties");
        rs.Open();

        int x = 0;

        while (mocEnum.MoveNext())
```

```csharp
            {
                rs.AddNew();
                ManagementBaseObject mo = mocEnum.Current;
                PropertyDataCollection props = mo.Properties;
                PropertyDataCollection.PropertyDataEnumerator
propEnum = props.GetEnumerator();
                while (propEnum.MoveNext())
                {
                    PropertyData prop = propEnum.Current;
                    try
                    {
                        rs.Fields[x].Value = GetValue(prop.Name,
mo);

                        x = x + 1;
                    }
                    catch (Exception ex)
                    {

                    }

                }
                x = 0;
                rs.Update();
            }

        }
        private System.String GetValue(System.String Name,
ManagementBaseObject mo)
        {
            int pos = 0;
            System.String tName = Name + " = ";
            System.String tempstr = mo.GetText(TextFormat.Mof);
            pos = tempstr.IndexOf(tName);
            if (pos > -1)
            {
                pos = pos + tName.Length;
                tempstr = tempstr.Substring(pos, tempstr.Length -
pos);
                pos = tempstr.IndexOf(";");
                tempstr = tempstr.Substring(0, pos);
                tempstr = tempstr.Replace("\"", "");
                tempstr = tempstr.Replace("{", "");
                tempstr = tempstr.Replace("}", "");
                if (mo.Properties[Name].Type == CimType.DateTime
&& tempstr.Length > 14)
```

```
                {
                    return tempstr.Substring(5, 2) + "/" +
tempstr.Substring(7, 2) + "/" + tempstr.Substring(0, 4) + " " +
tempstr.Substring(9, 2) + ":" + tempstr.Substring(11, 2) + ":" +
tempstr.Substring(13, 2);
                }
                else
                {
                    return tempstr;
                }
            }
            else
            {
                return "";
            }
        }
    }
}
```

Okay, so now that we've populated the table with information, let's start using it to create our first webpage using SQL Server.

```
            Class1 mchammer = new Class1();
            string tempstr = System.Environment.CurrentDirectory
+ "\\test.html";
            mchammer.Start_The_Show(tempstr,
"ProcessProperties");

mchammer.Write_The_Table_To_HTML("Provider=SQLOLEDB;Data
Source=.;Integrated Security=SSPI;Initial Catalog=Processes",
"ProcessProperties");
            mchammer.End_The_Show();
```

And the class code:

```
using System;
using System.Collections.Generic;
using System.Linq;
using System.Text;
using Scripting;
using System.Data.OleDb;

namespace WindowsFormsApplication2
```

```csharp
{
    class Class1
    {
        TextStream txtstream;
        public void Start_The_Show(string fName, string
tablename)
        {
            FileSystemObject fso = new FileSystemObject();
            txtstream = fso.OpenTextFile(fName,
IOMode.ForWriting, true, Tristate.TristateUseDefault);
            txtstream.WriteLine("<html>");
            txtstream.WriteLine("    <head>");
            txtstream.WriteLine("        <title>First
Page</title>");
            txtstream.WriteLine("            <style>");
            txtstream.WriteLine("            th");
            txtstream.WriteLine("            {");
            txtstream.WriteLine("                COLOR: white;");
            txtstream.WriteLine("                BACKGROUND-COLOR:
navy;");
            txtstream.WriteLine("                Font-family: Cambria,
serif;");
            txtstream.WriteLine("                FONT-SIZE: 12px;");
            txtstream.WriteLine("                text-align: left;");
            txtstream.WriteLine("                display:table-
cell;");
            txtstream.WriteLine("                white-Space:
nowrap;");
            txtstream.WriteLine("            }");
            txtstream.WriteLine("            td");
            txtstream.WriteLine("            {");
            txtstream.WriteLine("                color: black;");
            txtstream.WriteLine("                background-color:
white;");
            txtstream.WriteLine("                font-size:10px;");
            txtstream.WriteLine("                font-family:Calibri,
Sans-Serif;");
            txtstream.WriteLine("                display:table-
cell;");
            txtstream.WriteLine("                text-align: left");
            txtstream.WriteLine("                white-space:
nowrap;");
            txtstream.WriteLine("            }");
            txtstream.WriteLine("            table.main");
            txtstream.WriteLine("            {");
```

```
            txtstream.WriteLine("            border-color: navy;");
            txtstream.WriteLine("            border-width: 2px;");
            txtstream.WriteLine("            text-align: left");
            txtstream.WriteLine("        }");
            txtstream.WriteLine("        input");
            txtstream.WriteLine("        {");
            txtstream.WriteLine("            COLOR: black;");
            txtstream.WriteLine("            BACKGROUND-COLOR: white;");
            txtstream.WriteLine("            Font-family: Cambria, serif;");
            txtstream.WriteLine("            FONT-SIZE: 10px;");
            txtstream.WriteLine("            text-align: left");
            txtstream.WriteLine("            white-Space: nowrap;");
            txtstream.WriteLine("            width:100%;");
            txtstream.WriteLine("        }");
            txtstream.WriteLine("        .solid");
            txtstream.WriteLine("        {");
            txtstream.WriteLine("            width: 100%;");
            txtstream.WriteLine("            display: inline-block;");
            txtstream.WriteLine("        }");
            txtstream.WriteLine("        .double");
            txtstream.WriteLine("        {");
            txtstream.WriteLine("            border-style: double;");
            txtstream.WriteLine("        }");
            txtstream.WriteLine("        .ridge");
            txtstream.WriteLine("        {");
            txtstream.WriteLine("            border-style: ridge;");
            txtstream.WriteLine("        }");
            txtstream.WriteLine("        .inset");
            txtstream.WriteLine("        {");
            txtstream.WriteLine("            border-style: inset;");
            txtstream.WriteLine("        }");
            txtstream.WriteLine("        .groove");
            txtstream.WriteLine("        {");
            txtstream.WriteLine("            border-style: groove;");
            txtstream.WriteLine("        }");
            txtstream.WriteLine("        .dashed");
```

```csharp
            txtstream.WriteLine("            {");
            txtstream.WriteLine("                border-style:
dashed;");
            txtstream.WriteLine("            }");
            txtstream.WriteLine("            .dotted");
            txtstream.WriteLine("            {");
            txtstream.WriteLine("                border-style:
dotted;");
            txtstream.WriteLine("            }");
            txtstream.WriteLine("            .outset");
            txtstream.WriteLine("            {");
            txtstream.WriteLine("                border-style:
outset;");
            txtstream.WriteLine("            }");
            txtstream.WriteLine("            </style>");
            txtstream.WriteLine("        </head>");
            txtstream.WriteLine("        <body>");
        }
        public void Write_The_Table_To_HTML(string cnstr, string
tablename)
        {
            Array l;
            OleDbDataAdapter da = new OleDbDataAdapter("Select *
From " + tablename, cnstr);
            System.Data.DataTable dt = new
System.Data.DataTable();
            da.Fill(dt);

            int x = 0;
            l = Array.CreateInstance(typeof(int),
dt.Columns.Count);
            foreach (System.Data.DataColumn dc in dt.Columns)
            {
                l.SetValue(dc.Caption.Length, x);
                x = x + 1;
            }
            x = 0;
            foreach (System.Data.DataRow dr in dt.Rows)
            {
                foreach (System.Data.DataColumn dc in dt.Columns)
                {
                    int z = (int)l.GetValue(x);

                    if (z < dr[dc.Caption].ToString().Length)
                    {
```

```
l.SetValue(dr[dc.Caption].ToString().Length, x);
                }
                x = x + 1;
            }
            x = 0;
        }
        txtstream.WriteLine("             <table class =
\"table.main double\" frame=\"both\" rules=\"all\"
cellpadding=\"3px\" width=100%>");
        txtstream.WriteLine("                    <tr>");

        foreach (System.Data.DataColumn dc in dt.Columns)
        {
            int z = (int)l.GetValue(x);
            if (z == 0)
            {
                z = 20;
            }
            else
            {
                if (z < 10)
                {
                    z = z * 8;
                }
                else
                {
                    if (z < 30)
                    {
                        z = z * 7;
                    }
                    else
                    {
                        if (z < 50)
                        {
                            z = z * 6;
                        }
                        else
                        {
                            if (z < 70)
                            {
                                z = z * 5;
                            }
                            else
                            {
```

```csharp
                                        if (z < 90)
                                        {
                                            z = z * (int)4.5;
                                        }
                                        else
                                        {
                                            z = (z - 100) * 4;
                                        }
                                    }
                                }
                            }
                        }
                    }

                    txtstream.WriteLine("                          <th
style=\"width:" + z + "px\">" + dc.Caption + "</th>");
                    z = 0;
                    x = x + 1;
                }
                x = 0;
                txtstream.WriteLine("                          </tr>");

                foreach (System.Data.DataRow dr in dt.Rows)
                {
                    txtstream.WriteLine("                      <tr>");
                    foreach (System.Data.DataColumn dc in dt.Columns)
                    {
                        int z = (int)1.GetValue(x);
                        if (z == 0)
                        {
                            z = 20;
                        }
                        else
                        {
                            if (z < 10)
                            {
                                z = z * 8;
                            }
                            else
                            {
                                if (z < 30)
                                {
                                    z = z * 7;
                                }
                                else
```

```csharp
                    {
                        if (z < 50)
                        {
                            z = z * 6;
                        }
                        else
                        {
                            if (z < 90)
                            {
                                z = z * 5;
                            }
                            else
                            {
                                if (z < 200)
                                {
                                    z = z * (int)4;
                                }
                                else
                                {
                                    z = (z - 400) * 4;
                                }
                            }
                        }
                    }
                    try
                    {
                        txtstream.WriteLine("
<td><input type='text' Value='" + dr[dc.Caption].ToString() + "'
style=\"width:" + z + "px\"></input></td>");
                    }
                    catch (Exception ex)
                    {
                        txtstream.WriteLine("
<td><input type='text' style=\"width:" + z +
"px\"></input></td>");
                    }
                    z = 0;
                    x = x + 1;
                }
                txtstream.WriteLine("                        </tr>");
                x = 0;
            }
            txtstream.WriteLine("                    </tbody>");
```

```
            txtstream.WriteLine("          </table>");
        }
        public void End_The_Show()
        {
            txtstream.WriteLine("    </body>");
            txtstream.WriteLine("</html>");
            txtstream.Close();
        }
    }
}
```

The code above produced the HTML below:

Caption	CommandLine
System Idle Process	
System	
smss.exe	
csrss.exe	
wininit.exe	
csrss.exe	
winlogon.exe	winlogon.exe
services.exe	
lsass.exe	C:\\Windows\\system32\\lsass.exe
svchost.exe	C:\\Windows\\system32\\svchost.exe -k DcomLaunch
svchost.exe	C:\\Windows\\system32\\svchost.exe -k RPCSS
dwm.exe	\dwm.exe\
svchost.exe	C:\\Windows\\System32\\svchost.exe -k LocalSystemNetworkRestricted
NVDisplay.Container.exe	\C:\\Program Files\\NVIDIA Corporation\\Display.NvContainer\\NVDisplay.Container.exe\ -s NVD
svchost.exe	C:\\Windows\\System32\\svchost.exe -k LocalServiceNetworkRestricted
svchost.exe	C:\\Windows\\system32\\svchost.exe -k LocalServiceNoNetwork

I honestly don't think that it can get any easier then how I did this. The code isn't hardcore – like adding primary and foreign keys, creating more than one table and linking them, or creating specific data types to fields.

Anyway, once you now know how to create a SQL Server database and table and then populate it with data. All four routines to create HTML, HTA, ASP and ASPX files for the Access database – the proven code is in this book - can be used by your SQL Server database and the table you've created.

Simply change out the connection string from Access to SQL Server and replace the tablename from Properties to ProcessProperties.

STYLESHEET VISUALIZATIONS

What the stylesheets should look like when used

T he images below were captured to show you what the html will look like when they are added to the html.

Report:

Table

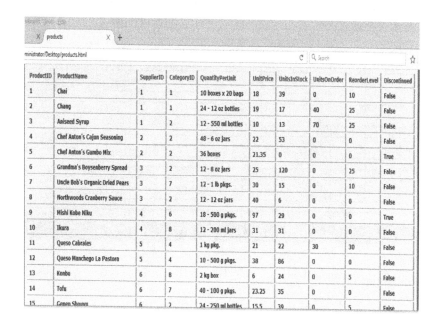

ProductID	ProductName	SupplierID	CategoryID	QuantityPerUnit	UnitPrice	UnitsInStock	UnitsOnOrder	ReorderLevel	Discontinued
1	Chai	1	1	10 boxes x 20 bags	18	39	0	10	False
2	Chang	1	1	24 - 12 oz bottles	19	17	40	25	False
3	Aniseed Syrup	1	2	12 - 550 ml bottles	10	13	70	25	False
4	Chef Anton's Cajun Seasoning	2	2	48 - 6 oz jars	22	53	0	0	False
5	Chef Anton's Gumbo Mix	2	2	36 boxes	21.35	0	0	0	True
6	Grandma's Boysenberry Spread	3	2	12 - 8 oz jars	25	120	0	25	False
7	Uncle Bob's Organic Dried Pears	3	7	12 - 1 lb pkgs.	30	15	0	10	False
8	Northwoods Cranberry Sauce	3	2	12 - 12 oz jars	40	6	0	0	False
9	Mishi Kobe Niku	4	6	18 - 500 g pkgs.	97	29	0	0	True
10	Ikura	4	8	12 - 200 ml jars	31	31	0	0	False
11	Queso Cabrales	5	4	1 kg pkg.	21	22	30	30	False
12	Queso Manchego La Pastora	5	4	10 - 500 g pkgs.	38	86	0	0	False
13	Konbu	6	8	2 kg box	6	24	0	5	False
14	Tofu	6	7	40 - 100 g pkgs.	23.25	35	0	0	False
15	Genen Shouyu	6	2	24 - 250 ml bottles	15.5	39	0	5	False

None:

Black and White

Colored:

AccountExpires	AuthorizationFlags	BadPasswordCount	Caption	CodePage	Comment	CountryCode	Description
			NT AUTHORITY\SYSTEM				Network login profile settings for SYSTEM on NT AUTHORITY
			NT AUTHORITY\LOCAL SERVICE				Network login profile settings for LOCAL SERVICE on NT AUTHORITY
			NT AUTHORITY\NETWORK SERVICE				Network login profile settings for NETWORK SERVICE on NT AUTHORITY
	0	0	Administrator	0	Built-in account for administering the computer/domain	0	Network login profile settings for on WIN-X3RLOAKMF5B
			NT SERVICE\SSASTELEMETRY				Network login profile settings for SSASTELEMETRY on NT SERVICE
			NT SERVICE\SSISTELEMETRY130				Network login profile settings for SSISTELEMETRY130 on NT SERVICE
			NT SERVICE\SQLTELEMETRY				Network login profile settings for SQLTELEMETRY on NT SERVICE
			NT SERVICE\MSSQLServerOLAPService				Network login profile settings for MSSQLServerOLAPService on NT SERVICE
			NT SERVICE\ReportServer				Network login profile settings for ReportServer on NT SERVICE
			NT SERVICE\MSSQLFDLauncher				Network login profile settings for MSSQLFDLauncher on NT SERVICE
			NT SERVICE\MSSQLLauncpad				Network login profile settings for MSSQLLaunchpad on NT SERVICE
			NT SERVICE\MsDtsServer130				Network login profile settings for MsDtsServer130 on NT SERVICE
			NT SERVICE\MSSQLSERVER				Network login profile settings for MSSQLSERVER on NT SERVICE
			IIS APPPOOL\Classic .NET AppPool				Network login profile settings for Classic .NET AppPool on IIS APPPOOL
			IIS APPPOOL\.NET v4.5				Network login profile settings for .NET v4.5 on IIS APPPOOL
			IIS APPPOOL\.NET v2.0				Network login profile settings for .NET v2.0 on IIS APPPOOL
			IIS APPPOOL\.NET v4.5 Classic				Network login profile settings for .NET v4.5 Classic on IIS APPPOOL
			IIS APPPOOL\.NET v2.0 Classic				Network login profile settings for .NET v2.0 Classic on IIS APPPOOL

Oscillating

Availability	BytesPerSector	Capabilities	CapabilityDescriptions	Caption	CompressionMethod	ConfigManagerErrorCode	ConfigManagerUserConfig
	512	3, 4, 10	Random Access, Supports Writing, SMART Notification	OCZ REVODRIVE350 SCSI Disk Device		0	FALSE
	512	3, 4	Random Access, Supports Writing	NVMe TOSHIBA-RD400		0	FALSE
	512	3, 4, 10	Random Access, Supports Writing, SMART Notification	TOSHIBA DT01ACA200		0	FALSE

:

3D

Availability	BytesPerSector	Capabilities	CapabilityDescriptions	Caption	CompressionMethod	ConfigManagerErrorCode	ConfigManagerUserConfig	CreationClassName
	512	3, 4, 10	Random Access, Supports Writing, SMART Notification	OCZ REVODRIVE350 SCSI Disk Device		0	FALSE	Win32_DiskDrive
	512	3, 4	Random Access, Supports Writing	NVMe TOSHIBA RD400		0	FALSE	Win32_DiskDrive
	512	3, 4, 10	Random Access, Supports Writing, SMART Notification	TOSHIBA DT01ACA200		0	FALSE	Win32_DiskDrive

Shadow Box:

Shadow Box Single Line Vertical

Shadow Box Multi line Vertical

Availability			
BytesPerSector	512	512	512
Capabilities	3, 4, 10	3, 4	3, 4, 10
CapabilityDescriptions	Random Access, Supports Writing, SMART Notification	Random Access, Supports Writing	Random Access, Supports Writing, SMART Notification
Caption	OCZ REVODRIVE350 SCSI Disk Device	NVMe TOSHIBA-RD400	TOSHIBA DT01ACA200
CompressionMethod			
ConfigManagerErrorCode	0	0	0
ConfigManagerUserConfig	FALSE	FALSE	FALSE
CreationClassName	Win32_DiskDrive	Win32_DiskDrive	Win32_DiskDrive
DefaultBlockSize			
Description	Disk drive	Disk drive	Disk drive
DeviceID	\\.\PHYSICALDRIVE2	\\.\PHYSICALDRIVE1	\\.\PHYSICALDRIVE0
ErrorCleared			
ErrorDescription			
ErrorMethodology			
FirmwareRevision	2.50	57CZ4102	MX4OABB0
Index	2	1	0

STYLESHEETS

Basic Stylesheets

Below are a collection of stylesheets you can use with any of the programs which use stylesheets.

You don't have to use them. They are just here for your consideration.

NONE

```
txtstream.WriteLine("<style type='text/css'>");
txtstream.WriteLine("th");
txtstream.WriteLine("{");
txtstream.WriteLine("    COLOR: white;");
txtstream.WriteLine("}");
txtstream.WriteLine("td");
txtstream.WriteLine("{");
txtstream.WriteLine("    COLOR: white;");
txtstream.WriteLine("}");
txtstream.WriteLine("</style>");
```

ITS A TABLE

```
txtstream.WriteLine("<style type='text/css'>");
txtstream.WriteLine("#itsthetable {");
```

```
        txtstream.WriteLine("        font-family: Georgia, """Times New Roman""",
Times, serif;");
        txtstream.WriteLine("        color: #036;");
        txtstream.WriteLine("}");
        txtstream.WriteLine("caption {");
        txtstream.WriteLine("        font-size: 48px;");
        txtstream.WriteLine("        color: #036;");
        txtstream.WriteLine("        font-weight: bolder;");
        txtstream.WriteLine("        font-variant: small-caps;");
        txtstream.WriteLine("}");
        txtstream.WriteLine("th {");
        txtstream.WriteLine("        font-size: 12px;");
        txtstream.WriteLine("        color: #FFF;");
        txtstream.WriteLine("        background-color: #06C;");
        txtstream.WriteLine("        padding: 8px 4px;");
        txtstream.WriteLine("        border-bottom: 1px solid #015ebc;");
        txtstream.WriteLine("}");
        txtstream.WriteLine("table {");
        txtstream.WriteLine("        margin: 0;");
        txtstream.WriteLine("        padding: 0;");
        txtstream.WriteLine("        border-collapse: collapse;");
        txtstream.WriteLine("        border: 1px solid #06C;");
        txtstream.WriteLine("        width: 100%");
        txtstream.WriteLine("}");
        txtstream.WriteLine("#itsthetable th a:link, #itsthetable th a:visited {");
        txtstream.WriteLine("        color: #FFF;");
        txtstream.WriteLine("        text-decoration: none;");
        txtstream.WriteLine("        border-left: 5px solid #FFF;");
        txtstream.WriteLine("        padding-left: 3px;");
        txtstream.WriteLine("}");
        txtstream.WriteLine("th a:hover, #itsthetable th a:active {");
        txtstream.WriteLine("        color: #F90;");
        txtstream.WriteLine("        text-decoration: line-through;");
        txtstream.WriteLine("        border-left: 5px solid #F90;");
        txtstream.WriteLine("        padding-left: 3px;");
        txtstream.WriteLine("}");
        txtstream.WriteLine("tbody th:hover {");
        txtstream.WriteLine("        background-image:
url(imgs/tbody_hover.gif);");
        txtstream.WriteLine("        background-position: bottom;");
```

```
txtstream.WriteLine("        background-repeat: repeat-x;");
txtstream.WriteLine("}");
txtstream.WriteLine("td {");
txtstream.WriteLine("        background-color: #f2f2f2;");
txtstream.WriteLine("        padding: 4px;");
txtstream.WriteLine("        font-size: 12px;");
txtstream.WriteLine("}");
txtstream.WriteLine("#itsthetable td:hover {");
txtstream.WriteLine("        background-color: #f8f8f8;");
txtstream.WriteLine("}");
txtstream.WriteLine("#itsthetable td a:link, #itsthetable td a:visited {");
txtstream.WriteLine("        color: #039;");
txtstream.WriteLine("        text-decoration: none;");
txtstream.WriteLine("        border-left: 3px solid #039;");
txtstream.WriteLine("        padding-left: 3px;");
txtstream.WriteLine("}");
txtstream.WriteLine("#itsthetable td a:hover, #itsthetable td a:active {");
txtstream.WriteLine("        color: #06C;");
txtstream.WriteLine("        text-decoration: line-through;");
txtstream.WriteLine("        border-left: 3px solid #06C;");
txtstream.WriteLine("        padding-left: 3px;");
txtstream.WriteLine("}");
txtstream.WriteLine("#itsthetable th {");
txtstream.WriteLine("        text-align: left;");
txtstream.WriteLine("        width: 150px;");
txtstream.WriteLine("}");
txtstream.WriteLine("#itsthetable tr {");
txtstream.WriteLine("        border-bottom: 1px solid #CCC;");
txtstream.WriteLine("}");
txtstream.WriteLine("#itsthetable thead th {");
txtstream.WriteLine("        background-image: url(imgs/thead_back.gif);");
txtstream.WriteLine("        background-repeat: repeat-x;");
txtstream.WriteLine("        background-color: #06C;");
txtstream.WriteLine("        height: 30px;");
txtstream.WriteLine("        font-size: 18px;");
txtstream.WriteLine("        text-align: center;");
txtstream.WriteLine("        text-shadow: #333 2px 2px;");
txtstream.WriteLine("        border: 2px;");
txtstream.WriteLine("}");
txtstream.WriteLine("#itsthetable tfoot th {");
```

```
txtstream.WriteLine("        background-image: url(imgs/tfoot_back.gif);");
txtstream.WriteLine("        background-repeat: repeat-x;");
txtstream.WriteLine("        background-color: #036;");
txtstream.WriteLine("        height: 30px;");
txtstream.WriteLine("        font-size: 28px;");
txtstream.WriteLine("        text-align: center;");
txtstream.WriteLine("        text-shadow: #333 2px 2px;");
txtstream.WriteLine("}");
txtstream.WriteLine("#itsthetable tfoot td {");
txtstream.WriteLine("        background-image: url(imgs/tfoot_back.gif);");
txtstream.WriteLine("        background-repeat: repeat-x;");
txtstream.WriteLine("        background-color: #036;");
txtstream.WriteLine("        color: FFF;");
txtstream.WriteLine("        height: 30px;");
txtstream.WriteLine("        font-size: 24px;");
txtstream.WriteLine("        text-align: left;");
txtstream.WriteLine("        text-shadow: #333 2px 2px;");
txtstream.WriteLine("}");
txtstream.WriteLine("tbody td a[href=""http://www.csslab.cl/""] {");
txtstream.WriteLine("        font-weight: bolder;");
txtstream.WriteLine("}");
txtstream.WriteLine("</style>");
```

BLACK AND WHITE TEXT

```
txtstream.WriteLine("<style type='text/css'>");
txtstream.WriteLine("th");
txtstream.WriteLine("{");
txtstream.WriteLine("    COLOR: white;");
txtstream.WriteLine("    BACKGROUND-COLOR: black;");
txtstream.WriteLine("    FONT-FAMILY:font-family: Cambria, serif;");
txtstream.WriteLine("    FONT-SIZE: 12px;");
txtstream.WriteLine("    text-align: left;");
txtstream.WriteLine("    white-Space: nowrap='nowrap';");
txtstream.WriteLine("}");
txtstream.WriteLine("td");
txtstream.WriteLine("{");
txtstream.WriteLine("    COLOR: white;");
txtstream.WriteLine("    BACKGROUND-COLOR: black;");
```

```
txtstream.WriteLine("    Font-family: Cambria, serif;");
txtstream.WriteLine("    FONT-SIZE: 12px;");
txtstream.WriteLine("    text-align: left;");
txtstream.WriteLine("    white-Space: nowrap='nowrap';");
txtstream.WriteLine("}");
txtstream.WriteLine("div");
txtstream.WriteLine("{");
txtstream.WriteLine("    COLOR: white;");
txtstream.WriteLine("    BACKGROUND-COLOR: black;");
txtstream.WriteLine("    Font-family: Cambria, serif;");
txtstream.WriteLine("    FONT-SIZE: 10px;");
txtstream.WriteLine("    text-align: left;");
txtstream.WriteLine("    white-Space: nowrap='nowrap';");
txtstream.WriteLine("}");
txtstream.WriteLine("span");
txtstream.WriteLine("{");
txtstream.WriteLine("    COLOR: white;");
txtstream.WriteLine("    BACKGROUND-COLOR: black;");
txtstream.WriteLine("    Font-family: Cambria, serif;");
txtstream.WriteLine("    FONT-SIZE: 10px;");
txtstream.WriteLine("    text-align: left;");
txtstream.WriteLine("    white-Space: nowrap='nowrap';");
txtstream.WriteLine("    display:inline-block;");
txtstream.WriteLine("    width: 100%;");
txtstream.WriteLine("}");
txtstream.WriteLine("textarea");
txtstream.WriteLine("{");
txtstream.WriteLine("    COLOR: white;");
txtstream.WriteLine("    BACKGROUND-COLOR: black;");
txtstream.WriteLine("    Font-family: Cambria, serif;");
txtstream.WriteLine("    FONT-SIZE: 10px;");
txtstream.WriteLine("    text-align: left;");
txtstream.WriteLine("    white-Space: nowrap='nowrap';");
txtstream.WriteLine("    width: 100%;");
txtstream.WriteLine("}");
txtstream.WriteLine("select");
txtstream.WriteLine("{");
txtstream.WriteLine("    COLOR: white;");
txtstream.WriteLine("    BACKGROUND-COLOR: black;");
txtstream.WriteLine("    Font-family: Cambria, serif;");
```

```
txtstream.WriteLine("  FONT-SIZE: 10px;");
txtstream.WriteLine("  text-align: left;");
txtstream.WriteLine("  white-Space: nowrap='nowrap';");
txtstream.WriteLine("  width: 100%;");
txtstream.WriteLine("}");
txtstream.WriteLine("input");
txtstream.WriteLine("{");
txtstream.WriteLine("  COLOR: white;");
txtstream.WriteLine("  BACKGROUND-COLOR: black;");
txtstream.WriteLine("  Font-family: Cambria, serif;");
txtstream.WriteLine("  FONT-SIZE: 12px;");
txtstream.WriteLine("  text-align: left;");
txtstream.WriteLine("  display:table-cell;");
txtstream.WriteLine("  white-Space: nowrap='nowrap';");
txtstream.WriteLine("}");
txtstream.WriteLine("h1 {");
txtstream.WriteLine("color: antiquewhite;");
txtstream.WriteLine("text-shadow: 1px 1px 1px black;");
txtstream.WriteLine("padding: 3px;");
txtstream.WriteLine("text-align: center;");
txtstream.WriteLine("box-shadow: inset 2px 2px 5px rgba(0,0,0,0.5), inset -2px -2px 5px rgba(255,255,255,0.5);");
txtstream.WriteLine("}");
txtstream.WriteLine("</style>");
```

Colored Text

```
txtstream.WriteLine("<style type='text/css'>");
txtstream.WriteLine("th");
txtstream.WriteLine("{");
txtstream.WriteLine("  COLOR: darkred;");
txtstream.WriteLine("  BACKGROUND-COLOR: #eeeeee;");
txtstream.WriteLine("  FONT-FAMILY:font-family: Cambria, serif;");
txtstream.WriteLine("  FONT-SIZE: 12px;");
txtstream.WriteLine("  text-align: left;");
txtstream.WriteLine("  white-Space: nowrap='nowrap';");
txtstream.WriteLine("}");
txtstream.WriteLine("td");
txtstream.WriteLine("{");
```

```
txtstream.WriteLine("    COLOR: navy;");
txtstream.WriteLine("    BACKGROUND-COLOR: #eeeeee;");
txtstream.WriteLine("    Font-family: Cambria, serif;");
txtstream.WriteLine("    FONT-SIZE: 12px;");
txtstream.WriteLine("    text-align: left;");
txtstream.WriteLine("    white-Space: nowrap='nowrap';");
txtstream.WriteLine("}");
txtstream.WriteLine("div");
txtstream.WriteLine("{");
txtstream.WriteLine("    COLOR: white;");
txtstream.WriteLine("    BACKGROUND-COLOR: navy;");
txtstream.WriteLine("    Font-family: Cambria, serif;");
txtstream.WriteLine("    FONT-SIZE: 10px;");
txtstream.WriteLine("    text-align: left;");
txtstream.WriteLine("    white-Space: nowrap='nowrap';");
txtstream.WriteLine("}");
txtstream.WriteLine("span");
txtstream.WriteLine("{");
txtstream.WriteLine("    COLOR: white;");
txtstream.WriteLine("    BACKGROUND-COLOR: navy;");
txtstream.WriteLine("    Font-family: Cambria, serif;");
txtstream.WriteLine("    FONT-SIZE: 10px;");
txtstream.WriteLine("    text-align: left;");
txtstream.WriteLine("    white-Space: nowrap='nowrap';");
txtstream.WriteLine("    display:inline-block;");
txtstream.WriteLine("    width: 100%;");
txtstream.WriteLine("}");
txtstream.WriteLine("textarea");
txtstream.WriteLine("{");
txtstream.WriteLine("    COLOR: white;");
txtstream.WriteLine("    BACKGROUND-COLOR: navy;");
txtstream.WriteLine("    Font-family: Cambria, serif;");
txtstream.WriteLine("    FONT-SIZE: 10px;");
txtstream.WriteLine("    text-align: left;");
txtstream.WriteLine("    white-Space: nowrap='nowrap';");
txtstream.WriteLine("    width: 100%;");
txtstream.WriteLine("}");
txtstream.WriteLine("select");
txtstream.WriteLine("{");
txtstream.WriteLine("    COLOR: white;");
```

```
txtstream.WriteLine("    BACKGROUND-COLOR: navy;");
txtstream.WriteLine("    Font-family: Cambria, serif;");
txtstream.WriteLine("    FONT-SIZE: 10px;");
txtstream.WriteLine("    text-align: left;");
txtstream.WriteLine("    white-Space: nowrap='nowrap';");
txtstream.WriteLine("    width: 100%;");
txtstream.WriteLine("}");
txtstream.WriteLine("input");
txtstream.WriteLine("{“);
txtstream.WriteLine("    COLOR: white;");
txtstream.WriteLine("    BACKGROUND-COLOR: navy;");
txtstream.WriteLine("    Font-family: Cambria, serif;");
txtstream.WriteLine("    FONT-SIZE: 12px;");
txtstream.WriteLine("    text-align: left;");
txtstream.WriteLine("    display:table-cell;");
txtstream.WriteLine("    white-Space: nowrap='nowrap';");
txtstream.WriteLine("}");
txtstream.WriteLine("h1 {“);
txtstream.WriteLine("color: antiquewhite;");
txtstream.WriteLine("text-shadow: 1px 1px 1px black;");
txtstream.WriteLine("padding: 3px;");
txtstream.WriteLine("text-align: center;");
txtstream.WriteLine("box-shadow: inset 2px 2px 5px rgba(0,0,0,0.5), inset
-2px -2px 5px rgba(255,255,255,0.5);");
txtstream.WriteLine("}");
txtstream.WriteLine("</style>“);
```

OSCILLATING ROW COLORS

```
txtstream.WriteLine("<style type='text/css'>“);
txtstream.WriteLine("th");
txtstream.WriteLine("{“);
txtstream.WriteLine("    COLOR: white;");
txtstream.WriteLine("    BACKGROUND-COLOR: navy;");
txtstream.WriteLine("    FONT-FAMILY:font-family: Cambria, serif;");
txtstream.WriteLine("    FONT-SIZE: 12px;");
txtstream.WriteLine("    text-align: left;");
txtstream.WriteLine("    white-Space: nowrap='nowrap';");
txtstream.WriteLine("}");
```

```
txtstream.WriteLine("td");
txtstream.WriteLine("{“);
txtstream.WriteLine("   COLOR: navy;");
txtstream.WriteLine("   Font-family: Cambria, serif;");
txtstream.WriteLine("   FONT-SIZE: 12px;");
txtstream.WriteLine("   text-align: left;");
txtstream.WriteLine("   white-Space: nowrap='nowrap';");
txtstream.WriteLine("}”);
txtstream.WriteLine("div");
txtstream.WriteLine("{“);
txtstream.WriteLine("   COLOR: navy;");
txtstream.WriteLine("   Font-family: Cambria, serif;");
txtstream.WriteLine("   FONT-SIZE: 12px;");
txtstream.WriteLine("   text-align: left;");
txtstream.WriteLine("   white-Space: nowrap='nowrap';");
txtstream.WriteLine("}”);
txtstream.WriteLine("span");
txtstream.WriteLine("{“);
txtstream.WriteLine("   COLOR: navy;");
txtstream.WriteLine("   Font-family: Cambria, serif;");
txtstream.WriteLine("   FONT-SIZE: 12px;");
txtstream.WriteLine("   text-align: left;");
txtstream.WriteLine("   white-Space: nowrap='nowrap';");
txtstream.WriteLine("   width: 100%;");
txtstream.WriteLine("}”);
txtstream.WriteLine("textarea");
txtstream.WriteLine("{“);
txtstream.WriteLine("   COLOR: navy;");
txtstream.WriteLine("   Font-family: Cambria, serif;");
txtstream.WriteLine("   FONT-SIZE: 12px;");
txtstream.WriteLine("   text-align: left;");
txtstream.WriteLine("   white-Space: nowrap='nowrap';");
txtstream.WriteLine("   display:inline-block;");
txtstream.WriteLine("   width: 100%;");
txtstream.WriteLine("}”);
txtstream.WriteLine("select");
txtstream.WriteLine("{“);
txtstream.WriteLine("   COLOR: navy;");
txtstream.WriteLine("   Font-family: Cambria, serif;");
txtstream.WriteLine("   FONT-SIZE: 10px;");
```

```
txtstream.WriteLine("    text-align: left;");
txtstream.WriteLine("    white-Space: nowrap='nowrap';");
txtstream.WriteLine("    display:inline-block;");
txtstream.WriteLine("    width: 100%;");
txtstream.WriteLine("}");
txtstream.WriteLine("input");
txtstream.WriteLine("{");
txtstream.WriteLine("    COLOR: navy;");
txtstream.WriteLine("    Font-family: Cambria, serif;");
txtstream.WriteLine("    FONT-SIZE: 12px;");
txtstream.WriteLine("    text-align: left;");
txtstream.WriteLine("    display:table-cell;");
txtstream.WriteLine("    white-Space: nowrap='nowrap';");
txtstream.WriteLine("}");
txtstream.WriteLine("h1 {");
txtstream.WriteLine("color: antiquewhite;");
txtstream.WriteLine("text-shadow: 1px 1px 1px black;");
txtstream.WriteLine("padding: 3px;");
txtstream.WriteLine("text-align: center;");
txtstream.WriteLine("box-shadow: inset 2px 2px 5px rgba(0,0,0,0.5), inset
-2px -2px 5px rgba(255,255,255,0.5);");
txtstream.WriteLine("}");
txtstream.WriteLine("tr:nth-child(even){background-color:#f2f2f2;}");
txtstream.WriteLine("tr:nth-child(odd){background-color:#cccccc;
color:#f2f2f2;}");
txtstream.WriteLine("</style>");
```

GHOST DECORATED

```
txtstream.WriteLine("<style type='text/css'>");
txtstream.WriteLine("th");
txtstream.WriteLine("{");
txtstream.WriteLine("    COLOR: black;");
txtstream.WriteLine("    BACKGROUND-COLOR: white;");
txtstream.WriteLine("    FONT-FAMILY:font-family: Cambria, serif;");
txtstream.WriteLine("    FONT-SIZE: 12px;");
txtstream.WriteLine("    text-align: left;");
txtstream.WriteLine("    white-Space: nowrap='nowrap';");
txtstream.WriteLine("}");
```

```
txtstream.WriteLine("td");
txtstream.WriteLine("{");
txtstream.WriteLine("   COLOR: black;");
txtstream.WriteLine("   BACKGROUND-COLOR: white;");
txtstream.WriteLine("   Font-family: Cambria, serif;");
txtstream.WriteLine("   FONT-SIZE: 12px;");
txtstream.WriteLine("   text-align: left;");
txtstream.WriteLine("   white-Space: nowrap='nowrap';");
txtstream.WriteLine("}");
txtstream.WriteLine("div");
txtstream.WriteLine("{");
txtstream.WriteLine("   COLOR: black;");
txtstream.WriteLine("   BACKGROUND-COLOR: white;");
txtstream.WriteLine("   Font-family: Cambria, serif;");
txtstream.WriteLine("   FONT-SIZE: 10px;");
txtstream.WriteLine("   text-align: left;");
txtstream.WriteLine("   white-Space: nowrap='nowrap';");
txtstream.WriteLine("}");
txtstream.WriteLine("span");
txtstream.WriteLine("{");
txtstream.WriteLine("   COLOR: black;");
txtstream.WriteLine("   BACKGROUND-COLOR: white;");
txtstream.WriteLine("   font-family: Cambria, serif;");
txtstream.WriteLine("   FONT-SIZE: 10px;");
txtstream.WriteLine("   text-align: left;");
txtstream.WriteLine("   white-Space: nowrap='nowrap';");
txtstream.WriteLine("   display:inline-block;");
txtstream.WriteLine("   width: 100%;");
txtstream.WriteLine("}");
txtstream.WriteLine("textarea");
txtstream.WriteLine("{");
txtstream.WriteLine("   COLOR: black;");
txtstream.WriteLine("   BACKGROUND-COLOR: white;");
txtstream.WriteLine("   Font-family: Cambria, serif;");
txtstream.WriteLine("   FONT-SIZE: 10px;");
txtstream.WriteLine("   text-align: left;");
txtstream.WriteLine("   white-Space: nowrap='nowrap';");
txtstream.WriteLine("   width: 100%;");
txtstream.WriteLine("}");
txtstream.WriteLine("select");
```

```
txtstream.WriteLine("{“);
txtstream.WriteLine("    COLOR: black;”);
txtstream.WriteLine("    BACKGROUND-COLOR: white;”);
txtstream.WriteLine("    Font-family: Cambria, serif;”);
txtstream.WriteLine("    FONT-SIZE: 10px;”);
txtstream.WriteLine("    text-align: left;”);
txtstream.WriteLine("    white-Space: nowrap='nowrap';”);
txtstream.WriteLine("    width: 100%;”);
txtstream.WriteLine("}”);
txtstream.WriteLine("input”);
txtstream.WriteLine("{“);
txtstream.WriteLine("    COLOR: black;”);
txtstream.WriteLine("    BACKGROUND-COLOR: white;”);
txtstream.WriteLine("    Font-family: Cambria, serif;”);
txtstream.WriteLine("    FONT-SIZE: 12px;”);
txtstream.WriteLine("    text-align: left;”);
txtstream.WriteLine("    display:table-cell;”);
txtstream.WriteLine("    white-Space: nowrap='nowrap';”);
txtstream.WriteLine("}”);
txtstream.WriteLine("h1 {“);
txtstream.WriteLine("color: antiquewhite;”);
txtstream.WriteLine("text-shadow: 1px 1px 1px black;”);
txtstream.WriteLine("padding: 3px;”);
txtstream.WriteLine("text-align: center;”);
txtstream.WriteLine("box-shadow: inset 2px 2px 5px rgba(0,0,0,0.5), inset
-2px -2px 5px rgba(255,255,255,0.5);”);
txtstream.WriteLine("}”);
txtstream.WriteLine("</style>“);
```

3D

```
txtstream.WriteLine("<style type='text/css'>“);
txtstream.WriteLine("body”);
txtstream.WriteLine("{“);
txtstream.WriteLine("    PADDING-RIGHT: 0px;”);
txtstream.WriteLine("    PADDING-LEFT: 0px;”);
txtstream.WriteLine("    PADDING-BOTTOM: 0px;”);
txtstream.WriteLine("    MARGIN: 0px;”);
txtstream.WriteLine("    COLOR: #333;”);
```

```
txtstream.WriteLine("   PADDING-TOP: 0px;");
txtstream.WriteLine("      FONT-FAMILY: verdana, arial, helvetica, sans-serif;");
txtstream.WriteLine("}");
txtstream.WriteLine("table");
txtstream.WriteLine("{");
txtstream.WriteLine("   BORDER-RIGHT: #999999 3px solid;");
txtstream.WriteLine("   PADDING-RIGHT: 6px;");
txtstream.WriteLine("   PADDING-LEFT: 6px;");
txtstream.WriteLine("   FONT-WEIGHT: Bold;");
txtstream.WriteLine("   FONT-SIZE: 14px;");
txtstream.WriteLine("   PADDING-BOTTOM: 6px;");
txtstream.WriteLine("   COLOR: Peru;");
txtstream.WriteLine("   LINE-HEIGHT: 14px;");
txtstream.WriteLine("   PADDING-TOP: 6px;");
txtstream.WriteLine("   BORDER-BOTTOM: #999 1px solid;");
txtstream.WriteLine("   BACKGROUND-COLOR: #eeeeee;");
txtstream.WriteLine("      FONT-FAMILY: verdana, arial, helvetica, sans-serif;");
txtstream.WriteLine("   FONT-SIZE: 12px;");
txtstream.WriteLine("}");
txtstream.WriteLine("th");
txtstream.WriteLine("{");
txtstream.WriteLine("   BORDER-RIGHT: #999999 3px solid;");
txtstream.WriteLine("   PADDING-RIGHT: 6px;");
txtstream.WriteLine("   PADDING-LEFT: 6px;");
txtstream.WriteLine("   FONT-WEIGHT: Bold;");
txtstream.WriteLine("   FONT-SIZE: 14px;");
txtstream.WriteLine("   PADDING-BOTTOM: 6px;");
txtstream.WriteLine("   COLOR: darkred;");
txtstream.WriteLine("   LINE-HEIGHT: 14px;");
txtstream.WriteLine("   PADDING-TOP: 6px;");
txtstream.WriteLine("   BORDER-BOTTOM: #999 1px solid;");
txtstream.WriteLine("   BACKGROUND-COLOR: #eeeeee;");
txtstream.WriteLine("   font-family: Cambria, serif;");
txtstream.WriteLine("   FONT-SIZE: 12px;");
txtstream.WriteLine("   text-align: left;");
txtstream.WriteLine("   white-Space: nowrap='nowrap';");
txtstream.WriteLine("}");
txtstream.WriteLine(".th");
```

```
txtstream.WriteLine("{“);
txtstream.WriteLine("    BORDER-RIGHT: #999999 2px solid;”);
txtstream.WriteLine("    PADDING-RIGHT: 6px;”);
txtstream.WriteLine("    PADDING-LEFT: 6px;”);
txtstream.WriteLine("    FONT-WEIGHT: Bold;”);
txtstream.WriteLine("    PADDING-BOTTOM: 6px;”);
txtstream.WriteLine("    COLOR: black;”);
txtstream.WriteLine("    PADDING-TOP: 6px;”);
txtstream.WriteLine("    BORDER-BOTTOM: #999 2px solid;”);
txtstream.WriteLine("    BACKGROUND-COLOR: #eeeeee;”);
txtstream.WriteLine("    Font-family: Cambria, serif;”);
txtstream.WriteLine("    FONT-SIZE: 10px;”);
txtstream.WriteLine("    text-align: right;”);
txtstream.WriteLine("    white-Space: nowrap='nowrap';”);
txtstream.WriteLine("}”);
txtstream.WriteLine("td”);
txtstream.WriteLine("{“);
txtstream.WriteLine("    BORDER-RIGHT: #999999 3px solid;”);
txtstream.WriteLine("    PADDING-RIGHT: 6px;”);
txtstream.WriteLine("    PADDING-LEFT: 6px;”);
txtstream.WriteLine("    FONT-WEIGHT: Normal;”);
txtstream.WriteLine("    PADDING-BOTTOM: 6px;”);
txtstream.WriteLine("    COLOR: navy;”);
txtstream.WriteLine("    LINE-HEIGHT: 14px;”);
txtstream.WriteLine("    PADDING-TOP: 6px;”);
txtstream.WriteLine("    BORDER-BOTTOM: #999 1px solid;”);
txtstream.WriteLine("    BACKGROUND-COLOR: #eeeeee;”);
txtstream.WriteLine("    Font-family: Cambria, serif;”);
txtstream.WriteLine("    FONT-SIZE: 12px;”);
txtstream.WriteLine("    text-align: left;”);
txtstream.WriteLine("    white-Space: nowrap='nowrap';”);
txtstream.WriteLine("}”);
txtstream.WriteLine("div”);
txtstream.WriteLine("{“);
txtstream.WriteLine("    BORDER-RIGHT: #999999 3px solid;”);
txtstream.WriteLine("    PADDING-RIGHT: 6px;”);
txtstream.WriteLine("    PADDING-LEFT: 6px;”);
txtstream.WriteLine("    FONT-WEIGHT: Normal;”);
txtstream.WriteLine("    PADDING-BOTTOM: 6px;”);
txtstream.WriteLine("    COLOR: white;”);
```

```
txtstream.WriteLine("   PADDING-TOP: 6px;");
txtstream.WriteLine("   BORDER-BOTTOM: #999 1px solid;");
txtstream.WriteLine("   BACKGROUND-COLOR: navy;");
txtstream.WriteLine("   Font-family: Cambria, serif;");
txtstream.WriteLine("   FONT-SIZE: 10px;");
txtstream.WriteLine("   text-align: left;");
txtstream.WriteLine("   white-Space: nowrap='nowrap';");
txtstream.WriteLine("}");
txtstream.WriteLine("span");
txtstream.WriteLine("{");
txtstream.WriteLine("   BORDER-RIGHT: #999999 3px solid;");
txtstream.WriteLine("   PADDING-RIGHT: 3px;");
txtstream.WriteLine("   PADDING-LEFT: 3px;");
txtstream.WriteLine("   FONT-WEIGHT: Normal;");
txtstream.WriteLine("   PADDING-BOTTOM: 3px;");
txtstream.WriteLine("   COLOR: white;");
txtstream.WriteLine("   PADDING-TOP: 3px;");
txtstream.WriteLine("   BORDER-BOTTOM: #999 1px solid;");
txtstream.WriteLine("   BACKGROUND-COLOR: navy;");
txtstream.WriteLine("   Font-family: Cambria, serif;");
txtstream.WriteLine("   FONT-SIZE: 10px;");
txtstream.WriteLine("   text-align: left;");
txtstream.WriteLine("   white-Space: nowrap='nowrap';");
txtstream.WriteLine("   display:inline-block;");
txtstream.WriteLine("   width: 100%;");
txtstream.WriteLine("}");
txtstream.WriteLine("textarea");
txtstream.WriteLine("{");
txtstream.WriteLine("   BORDER-RIGHT: #999999 3px solid;");
txtstream.WriteLine("   PADDING-RIGHT: 3px;");
txtstream.WriteLine("   PADDING-LEFT: 3px;");
txtstream.WriteLine("   FONT-WEIGHT: Normal;");
txtstream.WriteLine("   PADDING-BOTTOM: 3px;");
txtstream.WriteLine("   COLOR: white;");
txtstream.WriteLine("   PADDING-TOP: 3px;");
txtstream.WriteLine("   BORDER-BOTTOM: #999 1px solid;");
txtstream.WriteLine("   BACKGROUND-COLOR: navy;");
txtstream.WriteLine("   Font-family: Cambria, serif;");
txtstream.WriteLine("   FONT-SIZE: 10px;");
txtstream.WriteLine("   text-align: left;");
```

```
txtstream.WriteLine("    white-Space: nowrap='nowrap';");
txtstream.WriteLine("    width: 100%;");
txtstream.WriteLine("}");
txtstream.WriteLine("select");
txtstream.WriteLine("{“);
txtstream.WriteLine("    BORDER-RIGHT: #999999 3px solid;");
txtstream.WriteLine("    PADDING-RIGHT: 6px;");
txtstream.WriteLine("    PADDING-LEFT: 6px;");
txtstream.WriteLine("    FONT-WEIGHT: Normal;");
txtstream.WriteLine("    PADDING-BOTTOM: 6px;");
txtstream.WriteLine("    COLOR: white;");
txtstream.WriteLine("    PADDING-TOP: 6px;");
txtstream.WriteLine("    BORDER-BOTTOM: #999 1px solid;");
txtstream.WriteLine("    BACKGROUND-COLOR: navy;");
txtstream.WriteLine("    Font-family: Cambria, serif;");
txtstream.WriteLine("    FONT-SIZE: 10px;");
txtstream.WriteLine("    text-align: left;");
txtstream.WriteLine("    white-Space: nowrap='nowrap';");
txtstream.WriteLine("    width: 100%;");
txtstream.WriteLine("}");
txtstream.WriteLine("input");
txtstream.WriteLine("{“);
txtstream.WriteLine("    BORDER-RIGHT: #999999 3px solid;");
txtstream.WriteLine("    PADDING-RIGHT: 3px;");
txtstream.WriteLine("    PADDING-LEFT: 3px;");
txtstream.WriteLine("    FONT-WEIGHT: Bold;");
txtstream.WriteLine("    PADDING-BOTTOM: 3px;");
txtstream.WriteLine("    COLOR: white;");
txtstream.WriteLine("    PADDING-TOP: 3px;");
txtstream.WriteLine("    BORDER-BOTTOM: #999 1px solid;");
txtstream.WriteLine("    BACKGROUND-COLOR: navy;");
txtstream.WriteLine("    Font-family: Cambria, serif;");
txtstream.WriteLine("    FONT-SIZE: 12px;");
txtstream.WriteLine("    text-align: left;");
txtstream.WriteLine("    display:table-cell;");
txtstream.WriteLine("    white-Space: nowrap='nowrap';");
txtstream.WriteLine("    width: 100%;");
txtstream.WriteLine("}");
txtstream.WriteLine("h1 {“);
txtstream.WriteLine("color: antiquewhite;");
```

```
txtstream.WriteLine("text-shadow: 1px 1px 1px black;");
txtstream.WriteLine("padding: 3px;");
txtstream.WriteLine("text-align: center;");
txtstream.WriteLine("box-shadow: inset 2px 2px 5px rgba(0,0,0,0.5), inset
-2px -2px 5px rgba(255,255,255,0.5);");
txtstream.WriteLine("}");
txtstream.WriteLine("</style>");
```

SHADOW BOX

```
txtstream.WriteLine("<style type='text/css'>");
txtstream.WriteLine("body");
txtstream.WriteLine("{");
txtstream.WriteLine("   PADDING-RIGHT: 0px;");
txtstream.WriteLine("   PADDING-LEFT: 0px;");
txtstream.WriteLine("   PADDING-BOTTOM: 0px;");
txtstream.WriteLine("   MARGIN: 0px;");
txtstream.WriteLine("   COLOR: #333;");
txtstream.WriteLine("   PADDING-TOP: 0px;");
txtstream.WriteLine("      FONT-FAMILY: verdana, arial, helvetica, sans-
serif;");
txtstream.WriteLine("}");
txtstream.WriteLine("table");
txtstream.WriteLine("{");
txtstream.WriteLine("   BORDER-RIGHT: #999999 1px solid;");
txtstream.WriteLine("   PADDING-RIGHT: 1px;");
txtstream.WriteLine("   PADDING-LEFT: 1px;");
txtstream.WriteLine("   PADDING-BOTTOM: 1px;");
txtstream.WriteLine("   LINE-HEIGHT: 8px;");
txtstream.WriteLine("   PADDING-TOP: 1px;");
txtstream.WriteLine("   BORDER-BOTTOM: #999 1px solid;");
txtstream.WriteLine("   BACKGROUND-COLOR: #eeeeee;");
txtstream.WriteLine("
filter:progid:DXImageTransform.Microsoft.Shadow(color='silver',    Direction=135,
Strength=16)");
txtstream.WriteLine("}");
txtstream.WriteLine("th");
txtstream.WriteLine("{");
txtstream.WriteLine("   BORDER-RIGHT: #999999 3px solid;");
```

```
txtstream.WriteLine("    PADDING-RIGHT: 6px;");
txtstream.WriteLine("    PADDING-LEFT: 6px;");
txtstream.WriteLine("    FONT-WEIGHT: Bold;");
txtstream.WriteLine("    FONT-SIZE: 14px;");
txtstream.WriteLine("    PADDING-BOTTOM: 6px;");
txtstream.WriteLine("    COLOR: darkred;");
txtstream.WriteLine("    LINE-HEIGHT: 14px;");
txtstream.WriteLine("    PADDING-TOP: 6px;");
txtstream.WriteLine("    BORDER-BOTTOM: #999 1px solid;");
txtstream.WriteLine("    BACKGROUND-COLOR: #eeeeee;");
txtstream.WriteLine("    Font-family: Cambria, serif;");
txtstream.WriteLine("    FONT-SIZE: 12px;");
txtstream.WriteLine("    text-align: left;");
txtstream.WriteLine("    white-Space: nowrap='nowrap';");
txtstream.WriteLine("}");
txtstream.WriteLine(".th");
txtstream.WriteLine("{");
txtstream.WriteLine("    BORDER-RIGHT: #999999 2px solid;");
txtstream.WriteLine("    PADDING-RIGHT: 6px;");
txtstream.WriteLine("    PADDING-LEFT: 6px;");
txtstream.WriteLine("    FONT-WEIGHT: Bold;");
txtstream.WriteLine("    PADDING-BOTTOM: 6px;");
txtstream.WriteLine("    COLOR: black;");
txtstream.WriteLine("    PADDING-TOP: 6px;");
txtstream.WriteLine("    BORDER-BOTTOM: #999 2px solid;");
txtstream.WriteLine("    BACKGROUND-COLOR: #eeeeee;");
txtstream.WriteLine("    Font-family: Cambria, serif;");
txtstream.WriteLine("    FONT-SIZE: 10px;");
txtstream.WriteLine("    text-align: right;");
txtstream.WriteLine("    white-Space: nowrap='nowrap';");
txtstream.WriteLine("}");
txtstream.WriteLine("td");
txtstream.WriteLine("{");
txtstream.WriteLine("    BORDER-RIGHT: #999999 3px solid;");
txtstream.WriteLine("    PADDING-RIGHT: 6px;");
txtstream.WriteLine("    PADDING-LEFT: 6px;");
txtstream.WriteLine("    FONT-WEIGHT: Normal;");
txtstream.WriteLine("    PADDING-BOTTOM: 6px;");
txtstream.WriteLine("    COLOR: navy;");
txtstream.WriteLine("    LINE-HEIGHT: 14px;");
```

```
txtstream.WriteLine("    PADDING-TOP: 6px;");
txtstream.WriteLine("    BORDER-BOTTOM: #999 1px solid;");
txtstream.WriteLine("    BACKGROUND-COLOR: #eeeeee;");
txtstream.WriteLine("    Font-family: Cambria, serif;");
txtstream.WriteLine("    FONT-SIZE: 12px;");
txtstream.WriteLine("    text-align: left;");
txtstream.WriteLine("    white-Space: nowrap='nowrap';");
txtstream.WriteLine("}");
txtstream.WriteLine("div");
txtstream.WriteLine("{");
txtstream.WriteLine("    BORDER-RIGHT: #999999 3px solid;");
txtstream.WriteLine("    PADDING-RIGHT: 6px;");
txtstream.WriteLine("    PADDING-LEFT: 6px;");
txtstream.WriteLine("    FONT-WEIGHT: Normal;");
txtstream.WriteLine("    PADDING-BOTTOM: 6px;");
txtstream.WriteLine("    COLOR: white;");
txtstream.WriteLine("    PADDING-TOP: 6px;");
txtstream.WriteLine("    BORDER-BOTTOM: #999 1px solid;");
txtstream.WriteLine("    BACKGROUND-COLOR: navy;");
txtstream.WriteLine("    Font-family: Cambria, serif;");
txtstream.WriteLine("    FONT-SIZE: 10px;");
txtstream.WriteLine("    text-align: left;");
txtstream.WriteLine("    white-Space: nowrap='nowrap';");
txtstream.WriteLine("}");
txtstream.WriteLine("span");
txtstream.WriteLine("{");
txtstream.WriteLine("    BORDER-RIGHT: #999999 3px solid;");
txtstream.WriteLine("    PADDING-RIGHT: 3px;");
txtstream.WriteLine("    PADDING-LEFT: 3px;");
txtstream.WriteLine("    FONT-WEIGHT: Normal;");
txtstream.WriteLine("    PADDING-BOTTOM: 3px;");
txtstream.WriteLine("    COLOR: white;");
txtstream.WriteLine("    PADDING-TOP: 3px;");
txtstream.WriteLine("    BORDER-BOTTOM: #999 1px solid;");
txtstream.WriteLine("    BACKGROUND-COLOR: navy;");
txtstream.WriteLine("    Font-family: Cambria, serif;");
txtstream.WriteLine("    FONT-SIZE: 10px;");
txtstream.WriteLine("    text-align: left;");
txtstream.WriteLine("    white-Space: nowrap='nowrap';");
txtstream.WriteLine("    display: inline-block;");
```

```
txtstream.WriteLine("    width: 100%;");
txtstream.WriteLine("}");
txtstream.WriteLine("textarea");
txtstream.WriteLine("{");
txtstream.WriteLine("    BORDER-RIGHT: #999999 3px solid;");
txtstream.WriteLine("    PADDING-RIGHT: 3px;");
txtstream.WriteLine("    PADDING-LEFT: 3px;");
txtstream.WriteLine("    FONT-WEIGHT: Normal;");
txtstream.WriteLine("    PADDING-BOTTOM: 3px;");
txtstream.WriteLine("    COLOR: white;");
txtstream.WriteLine("    PADDING-TOP: 3px;");
txtstream.WriteLine("    BORDER-BOTTOM: #999 1px solid;");
txtstream.WriteLine("    BACKGROUND-COLOR: navy;");
txtstream.WriteLine("    Font-family: Cambria, serif;");
txtstream.WriteLine("    FONT-SIZE: 10px;");
txtstream.WriteLine("    text-align: left;");
txtstream.WriteLine("    white-Space: nowrap='nowrap';");
txtstream.WriteLine("    width: 100%;");
txtstream.WriteLine("}");
txtstream.WriteLine("select");
txtstream.WriteLine("{");
txtstream.WriteLine("    BORDER-RIGHT: #999999 3px solid;");
txtstream.WriteLine("    PADDING-RIGHT: 6px;");
txtstream.WriteLine("    PADDING-LEFT: 6px;");
txtstream.WriteLine("    FONT-WEIGHT: Normal;");
txtstream.WriteLine("    PADDING-BOTTOM: 6px;");
txtstream.WriteLine("    COLOR: white;");
txtstream.WriteLine("    PADDING-TOP: 6px;");
txtstream.WriteLine("    BORDER-BOTTOM: #999 1px solid;");
txtstream.WriteLine("    BACKGROUND-COLOR: navy;");
txtstream.WriteLine("    Font-family: Cambria, serif;");
txtstream.WriteLine("    FONT-SIZE: 10px;");
txtstream.WriteLine("    text-align: left;");
txtstream.WriteLine("    white-Space: nowrap='nowrap';");
txtstream.WriteLine("    width: 100%;");
txtstream.WriteLine("}");
txtstream.WriteLine("input");
txtstream.WriteLine("{");
txtstream.WriteLine("    BORDER-RIGHT: #999999 3px solid;");
txtstream.WriteLine("    PADDING-RIGHT: 3px;");
```

```
txtstream.WriteLine("   PADDING-LEFT: 3px;");
txtstream.WriteLine("   FONT-WEIGHT: Bold;");
txtstream.WriteLine("   PADDING-BOTTOM: 3px;");
txtstream.WriteLine("   COLOR: white;");
txtstream.WriteLine("   PADDING-TOP: 3px;");
txtstream.WriteLine("   BORDER-BOTTOM: #999 1px solid;");
txtstream.WriteLine("   BACKGROUND-COLOR: navy;");
txtstream.WriteLine("   Font-family: Cambria, serif;");
txtstream.WriteLine("   FONT-SIZE: 12px;");
txtstream.WriteLine("   text-align: left;");
txtstream.WriteLine("   display: table-cell;");
txtstream.WriteLine("   white-Space: nowrap='nowrap';");
txtstream.WriteLine("   width: 100%;");
txtstream.WriteLine("}");
txtstream.WriteLine("h1 {");
txtstream.WriteLine("color: antiquewhite;");
txtstream.WriteLine("text-shadow: 1px 1px 1px black;");
txtstream.WriteLine("padding: 3px;");
txtstream.WriteLine("text-align: center;");
txtstream.WriteLine("box-shadow: inset 2px 2px 5px rgba(0,0,0,0.5), inset
-2px -2px 5px rgba(255,255,255,0.5);");
txtstream.WriteLine("}");
txtstream.WriteLine("</style>");
```

IN CONCLUSION

We've covered a lot of ground

What we have covered may come across to some of you as being simple but to the point. Which is exactly what I wanted to do.

But there is also something here that is fundamentally and strategically important. It is the basis for self-employment and the door opener for jobs throughout the world. I know I'm repeating myself as this was part of the introduction.

Think about it for a moment. You can now grab an ASP.Net book using C#.Net as the code behind language and build some awesome programs from what was covered in this book.

Anyway, try the code, watch it work and then add your own spin to each aspect of the code where it can be added to, modified or deleted. But above all, have fun!

ABOUT THIS AUTHOR

Richard T. Edwards is a self-taught programmer whose journey began back in 1995. He worked for Microsoft in technical support between 1996 and 2002.

After taking a bit of a break, he came back to Microsoft and started his programming career by writing a content management program for the games group.

But Windows Management Instrumentation (WMI) caught his attention back in 1999. After that, as they say, the rest is history.

From 2007 to current, Edwards has worked with Management Packs for System Center Operations Manager and System Center Service Manager. He tested and worked documentation on System Center Configuration Manager so that it could be installed on the Phoenix Domain at Microsoft. That domain now manages over 90,000 machines.

Edwards has worked for McDonalds, Ericson, Nuveen Investments, Caterpillar, United Health Care, Liberty Mutual, and Federal Home Loan Bank.

ADDITIONAL BOOKS YOU MIGHT ENJOY

Richard T. Edwards has over 670 book titles for you to consider. Below are the top 60 you can purchase through Amazon:

C++.Net and ODBC: Working with the Dataset
C++.Net and ODBC: Working with the DataTable
C++.Net and ODBC: Working with the DataView
C++.Net and OLEDB: Working with the Dataset
C++.Net and OLEDB: Working with the DataTable
C++.Net and OLEDB: Working with the DataView
C++.Net and SQL Client: Working with the Dataset
C++.Net and SQL Client: Working with the DataTable
C++.Net and SQL Client: Working with the DataView

C#.Net and ODBC: Working with the Dataset
C#.Net and ODBC: Working with the DataTable
C#.Net and ODBC: Working with the DataView
C#.Net and OLEDB: Working with the Dataset
C#.Net and OLEDB: Working with the DataTable
C#.Net and OLEDB: Working with the DataView
C#.Net and SQL Client: Working with the Dataset
C#.Net and SQL Client: Working with the DataTable
C#.Net and SQL Client: Working with the DataView

C#.Net and the WPF ListView: Using WMI in Async mode to power the Listview

C#.Net and the WPF DataGrid: Using WMI to power the DataGrid

C#.Net and the WPF DataGrid: Working with WMI Async

Inside VB.Net: Working with WMI and the WPF DataGrid

PowerShell and ODBC: Working with the Dataset

PowerShell and ODBC: Working with the DataTable

PowerShell and ODBC: Working with the DataView

PowerShell and OLEDB: Working with the Dataset

PowerShell and OLEDB: Working with the DataTable

PowerShell and OLEDB: Working with the DataView

PowerShell and SQL Client: Working with the Dataset

PowerShell and SQL Client: Working with the DataTable

PowerShell and SQL Client: Working with the DataView

Powershell and Get–WMIObject

Powershell and COM ADO

Powershell and COM DAO

Powershell and COM ODBC

PowerShell Without the Shell Shock

Powershell Programming in a book

Python Code Warrior – Doing DAO with Gusto

Python Code Warrior-Working with WMI

Simply JScript

Simply Kixtart

Simply PowerShell

Simply Python

Simply Rexx

Simply Ruby

Simply VB6

VB6 Source Code: Winmgmts ExecNotificationQuery: ___InstanceModificationEvent

VB.Net and ODBC: Working with the Dataset
VB.Net and ODBC: Working with the DataTable
VB.Net and ODBC: Working with the DataView
VB.Net and OLEDB: Working with the Dataset
VB.Net and OLEDB: Working with the DataTable
VB.Net and OLEDB: Working with the DataView
VB.Net and SQL Client: Working with the Dataset
VB.Net and SQL Client: Working with the DataTable
VB.Net and SQL Client: Working with the DataView

VB.Net and the Registry
VB.Net and COM ODBC: Working with the ADO and ODBC Drivers
VB.Net Database Essentials

VS 2017 AND WPF DATAGRID XML DRIVEN APPLICATION: Includes examples using Attribute, Element and Schema XML